I0112362

THE TRUTH ABOUT
the
BIG LIE
ADDICTS AND THOSE WHO LOVE THEM

THE TRUTH ABOUT
the
BIG LIE

ADDICTS AND THOSE WHO LOVE THEM

DWIGHT PLEDGER

SECOND EDITION

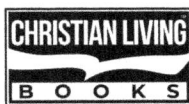

CHRISTIAN LIVING
B O O K S

Largo, MD

© Copyright 2020 Dwight Pledger

All rights reserved under the international copyright law. No part of this book may be reproduced or transmitted in any form or by any means, electronic or mechanical, including photocopying, recording, or by any information storage and retrieval system, without the express, written permission of the publisher or the author. The exception is reviewers, who may quote brief passages in a review.

ISBN 9781562295042

Christian Living Books, Inc.
P. O. Box 7584
Largo, MD 20792
christianlivingbooks.com
We bring your dreams to fruition.

Scriptures taken from the Holy Bible, New International Version®, NIV®. Copyright © 1973, 1978, 1984, 2011 by Biblica, Inc.® Used by permission of Zondervan. All rights reserved worldwide.

Contents

Foreword

AS HE STRETCHED OUT his arm with his head held back and eyes closed, Dwight Pledger took a deep breath while his friend injected the cocaine into his vein, an amount four times his usual fix, putting a demand on his heart that could result in shutting it down. Moments before losing consciousness, a lifetime of memories flashed before him, loving images of his wife and children. Dwight attempted to curl up on the floor and possibly close his eyes for the last time.

Once a great husband, proud father, and up-and-coming entrepreneur, now an out-of-control drug-dealing crack addict sprawled out on the floor in a drug-infested neighborhood of Oakland, California. Death pacing back and forth, smiling, excited, and anxiously waiting to take his soul, but because of God's grace and mercy, the story didn't end there.

My friend and mentor,
Mr. Les Brown, 2012.

With a spiritual elegance and gut-wrenching honesty, Dwight Pledger takes us on a frightening ride through

the valley of the shadow of death. He lost everything that meant anything to him, all because of one moment of indiscretion in the kitchen of a friend's house. By the grace of God, he was able to course-correct. Because of the prayers of Dwight's mother, wife, family, and friends who loved him, he refused to give up hope that he would one day be forever free.

Dwight has proven what author, Willie Jolley said, "A setback is a set up for a comeback." He has demonstrated that the power of a made-up mind can do incredible things. He walks us through the pages of his life to teach us that we, too, have comeback power.

This book will change your life.

Dwight, you have done us proud. God bless the day you were born.

—**Les Brown**
Motivational Speaker | Leading Authority on Achievement

Preface

DRUGS ARE DESTROYING MULTIPLE generations in America and abroad. This destruction is not limited to any age group, race, or socioeconomic status. I have seen what addiction has done to destroy the lives and careers of professional athletes, lawyers, wealthy businessmen, mothers, fathers, sisters, and brothers. Substance abuse has taken the lives of many of my friends, some of whom are serving long prison terms; others who will never recover from the deterioration of their minds caused by the excessive use of a myriad of drugs.

God only knows how I managed to survive my seven-year ordeal. This is the true account of how I allowed crack cocaine to destroy my home, career, and vital relationships. On several occasions, drugs almost caused me to lose my life. Mine is a story of how I was set free from the denial, guilt, and shame of my poor choices in life. It is the story of how I learned the truth about "The Big Lie" the hard way. I literally experienced what Warren Buffet meant, when he said, "The chains of habit are too light to be felt until they are too heavy to be broken."

This is a detailed blueprint of how "The Big Lie" played out in my life and how I eventually learned the truth that set me on my current path of change, transformation, and ongoing restoration.

Even if you have been blessed to avoid the trap of addiction, you will gain valuable insights that will help you to better understand why someone you love struggles with addiction. Not only will you have a better grasp of the problem, but I will leave no doubt about the solution that is available to all who have a sincere desire to be made forever free.

Introduction

YOU MIGHT BE ASKING, "What is 'The Big Lie'?" It is a series of lies that, when believed, will lead a person down a destructive pathway and to a life of misery, pain, and addiction. That journey will take them further than they want to go and keep them longer than they want to stay. This is an account of how I fell prey to seven big lies before finding the one truth that set me free:

1. It will never happen to me.
2. I'm only going to try it once.
3. I can quit anytime I want.
4. I've got everything under control.
5. I am not an addict.
6. I'm only hurting myself.
7. There is no hope for me.

When I saw and heard stories of people getting addicted to drugs, and destroying their lives, I believed Big Lie #1, "It will never happen to me." Believing that lie gave me a false sense of security and caused me to let down my guard. This set me up for Big Lie #2, "I'm only going to try it once." In the summer of 1979 when I was offered a "hit" of freebase cocaine, instead of saying, "No," I said, "Yes." Before," and before the year ended, I was hopelessly addicted.

While all signs in my life were pointing to the fact that I had a real big problem, I told myself, Big Lie #3, "I can quit anytime I want." Unable to control the monster I had created, I selfishly chose to believe Big Lie #4, "I've got everything under control." The reality was that my life was out of control. I couldn't stop getting high, no matter how hard I tried. Pride and shame made me desperate to believe, Big Lie #5, "I'm not an addict." Yet, in the face of everything pointing to my addictive lifestyle, I refused to admit that I was an addict.

Denial is a very strong force that kept me in bondage and allowed me to believe Big Lie #6, "I'm only hurting myself." My addiction was negatively impacting several vital relationships, not to mention the countless number of lives I helped to destroy by selling them death and destruction. Accepting this harsh reality caused me to believe the biggest of all lies, Big Lie #7, "There is no hope for me." This lie gave me an excuse to surrender and give up fighting for my freedom. I began to believe that if I could not beat it, I might as well give over to it. This "Big Lie" kept me trapped for many more years until I surfaced from the depths of deception and realized the truth: there was hope for me.

Throughout this book, you will discover how those seven lies impacted the trajectory of my life, and how I was finally brought face to face with the ultimate truth that made me free. I learned that I did not have to remain a slave to my addiction. I learned that it was possible to break the chains of habit and be made free which as you will discover is *The Truth About The Big Lie.*

One

Everything Is Under Control

S TANDING IN THE KITCHEN of a friend's house in Southeast San Diego, California, I watched as her friend poured the contents of a little brown bottle onto the screens of his freebase pipe. I stared intently as he put the fire to the screens, and the smoke began to fill the glass pipe. He took in a long continuous puff. I can vividly recall the confused look on his face after he blew out a steady stream of smoke, and then gasped as if he was trying to catch his breath. I was curious to try it "just once."

I remember it cost twenty-five dollars for just one "hit" off the pipe. I inhaled as much as I could and let the smoke trail out slowly. I didn't feel anything special. Since it had no profound effect on me, I thought to myself, "I can handle this drug." Of course, that was part of the Big Lie. I didn't know it then, but I would regret that day for the rest of my life. It was Warren Buffet who said, "The chains of habit are too light to be felt until they are too heavy to be broken." Truer words could not have been spoken, because before that year ended, I would be hopelessly addicted to smoking crack cocaine.

That was the beginning of the end of life as I knew it. A few questions I've asked myself are: Was I a victim or part of the problem? Was this a predictable outcome due to my upbringing? How does my story fit into the war on drugs? How did I get to that point? And after I got to that point what happened following that first time? I will answer these and other questions as they relate to the war on drugs that I lost. True recovery requires looking back with integrity and taking ownership of our choices.

Growing up in Redlands, California afforded me a relatively normal childhood. I was raised by a very loving mother, in a close-knit family of five girls and two boys. Economically, we were considered members of the lower class because we received public assistance, also known as welfare. But, to my mother's credit, I never once went hungry while under her roof.

During my high school years, I was preoccupied with after school sports. Among my peers, I was considered straight-laced because I didn't participate in many of their drug-related activities. Many of them smoked weed and used speed and LSD. I thought that anyone who used drugs was stupid, so I occupied my time with extracurricular activities. I was president of Redlands Senior High School's Black Student Union and I was inducted to our school's Track and Field Hall of Fame.

The Devil's Playground

After graduating from high school, with too much time on my hands, I soon gave into peer pressure. I started smoking marijuana and taking "mini bennies" (a form of amphetamines). Jobless, I was always in the streets hanging out with my friends and getting into some kind of mischief. The police were constantly coming to the house asking questions about me.

Seeing what I was becoming, one day mama called me into her bedroom and said, "Son, I love you, but you have got to go!" Less than six months later I enlisted in the U.S. Navy, which at that time was the best decision I could have made. Following basic training, I was shipped out to the Philippine Islands, eight thousand miles away. My ship, the USS Hassayampa AO-145, was on a Western-Pacific deployment.

I tried to stretch Mama's apron strings the entire eight thousand miles. I was very homesick, so one day I went to the chaplain's office. While there I became emotional. I told the chaplain that I needed to go home to my mother because she needed me. The chaplain gave me a look of disgust and told me to get out of his office and go back to work. I thought to myself, "That was not very loving of him to treat me like that." I soon made a few friends on the ship, and it wasn't long before I ran into the druggies. I began smoking weed, dropping speed, and taking LSD. Of course, I had "everything under control."

After returning to Pearl Harbor, which was the home port for my ship, I got into the routine of Navy life. The amount of money I was making as an E-2 didn't go very far on Oahu Island, which was a very expensive place to live. I would usually hitchhike to and from Waikiki Beach.

In my Navy Dress Blues in 1971.

My Beautiful Sadie

I spent a lot of time talking on the phone with my childhood sweetheart, Sadie, who was a senior in high school. I was basically a loner preferring not to run with the pack. I would get high every now and then to take the edge off, but of course, I had "everything under control."

Finally, the day came when I was able to take some leave time, so I went to Redlands, California. Sadie was graduating and I wanted to attend the ceremony. While in Redlands I was able to spend some quality time with Sadie and we decided to get married. We went to Gordon's Jeweler in downtown Redlands, where we bought a nice set of rings on credit. After obtaining a marriage license in San Diego, we arranged for the Navy chaplain to perform the ceremony at the North Chapel.

June 15, 1972, was a day like no other in that Sadie not only would be graduating from High School, but we would also travel to San Diego, and be joined together as husband and wife. We got up that morning and my friend, Steve Wimberly, drove us one hundred and ten miles to the Naval Training Center Chapel. After arriving we met with the chaplain, presented our marriage license, and were informed that we needed two witnesses. We were one witness short. The chaplain could not proceed without a second witness. I had to think of something fast. I ran across the street to the Base Exchange Store. As I was walking through the store, I saw a high school friend

> *I was considered straight-laced because I didn't participate in drug-related activities.*

named, Fred Jensen. I walked up to Fred, told him my situation, and he agreed to come across the street to stand in as our second witness. Sadie and I exchanged our vows, which ended with the words, "Until death do us part." Over the course of time, those words would surely be tested.

Immediately after the ceremony, we had to drive back to Redlands for Sadie's graduation ceremony. The drive back seemed surreal in that I was trying to wrap my head around what just happened. Sadie and I were now husband and wife, for better, for worse, for richer, for poorer. Did either of us understand what we had just committed to? Again, time would answer that question.

I wish I could say that after the graduation we departed for an exotic honeymoon, but that was not the case. I was due to

> *Did either of us understand what we had just committed to?*

report back to my ship, which was docked in Pearl Harbor. Neither one of us was ready to say good-bye, but as they say, "Duty called!" I soon returned to my ship and got back into the routine of Navy life. It would be a few months before I would see my wife again, and I could hardly wait. I remember closing all of my letters to Sadie with the words, "Someday, we will be together again!"

Brighter Days

Beau, a fellow shipmate, was renting an apartment in Waikiki Beach, just two blocks from the Ilikai Hotel. Beau didn't want to continue paying rent and decided to allow me to take over his place. It would take nearly all of my paycheck, but it meant that Sadie would be able to join me in Hawaii. What a place to spend the first year of marriage! It was a one-bedroom kitchenette, but to us, it would be "Home Sweet Home."

We had a ball in that little apartment. It was just a couple of blocks from the beach and not far from the International Market Place in Waikiki Village. For a while, I had to hitchhike back and forth to Pearl Harbor where my ship was docked. We managed to purchase a 1959 Chevy Impala. It rode like a Cadillac to us. We went all over the island in that car, until it stopped running and we left it on the side of the road somewhere on Oahu. We definitely got our money's worth out of that old Chevy. Sadie eventually had to return to California, but it wouldn't be long before we would be together again.

I was transferred from Hawaii due to an allergic reaction to some of the plants and trees in Hawaii. The vegetation triggered my childhood asthma. I was given a medical transfer to the Naval Air Station located in Imperial Beach, California. After arriving in the San Diego area, I limited my drug use to smoking weed and taking a little speed every now and then.

> Of course, I had "everything under control."

Of course, I had "everything under control." This brings me to one of the significant misconceptions or "Big Lies" a drug user believes about their habit, which is that they have everything under control, which of course is not true.

I soon grew tired of smoking marijuana and one day abruptly quit smoking it. I went on a self-improvement binge. I had been in the Navy for over two years and was beginning to advance in rank at a relatively fast rate. I was constantly on the go, working during the day, and attending school four nights a week. To maintain my productivity, the methamphetamine known as speed, became my main high. I used it on the weekends, usually going without any sleep. Oblivious to the beast hibernating beneath the surface of my life, I began my short-lived road to success and life in the fast lane.

The Second

On May 2, 1975, while in Imperial Beach, we were blessed with our first child, a boy, so of course I named him Dwight D. Pledger II. That day was one of the happiest days of my life, dampened only by his three-week stay in the hospital due to a condition called hyper-bilirubinemia. Needless to say, we didn't miss a day going to see him until the day we brought him home.

I was later transferred to Naval Air Station North Island. While there, I developed a keen interest in real estate, subsequently earned my real estate license, and began working part-time for Century 21 Realty in Imperial Beach. As my income increased, I began to move up the proverbial ladder of success.

My promotion to First Class Personnelman with Petty Officer Souza, at Naval Air Reserve Unit, Coronado, CA in 1977

I was also participating in the Navy's sports program and frequently traveled to various cities and states. So, as you can see, I had a rather busy schedule, but one way I was able to keep up with my busy schedule was to take a little speed more often than usual. Of course, I thought I had, "everything under control," but I didn't. At the time, I felt that I was progressing at a very rapid pace and my future looked promising… on the surface. Only in looking back on those days can I now see that I was a drug problem waiting for a life to destroy, not knowing that the life would be my own.

Two

The Toothpick Castle

IN 1978 I WAS finally discharged from the Navy with an honorable discharge and a rank of E-6, and I continued to progress in my real estate career with a steadily increasing income. I was working with single-family re-sales and income property investors. The real estate market in San Diego was hot. On the surface it looked like the boy from the projects in Redlands, California was going to be alright. It was then that things really started to move into high gear. It seemed as if the good times would never end. I remember that my favorite song by McFadden and Whitehead declared, "Ain't no stoppin' us now; we're on the move!"

About this time, my mother came to visit us at our home in Lemon Grove, California. Even though my mother was happy about our success, she could see that my lifestyle wasn't pleasing to God. Mama would always share something about her faith in the Lord. She would encourage me to start serving God and pay tithes to God for the many blessings He had bestowed on my family.

I was like so many other so-called self-made successes, who ended up worshipping their creator, which, in this case, was me. I couldn't understand how she could expect me to give $500 to $600 at a time to a church. It just didn't make a bit of sense to me at the time. Only in looking back can I see that I should have taken her advice. I was blinded by pride and driven by my toxic ego.

The Illusion of Control

As the next few years went by, success continued to follow me. I was always in the right place at the right time to connect with some of the movers and shakers in the San Diego social scene. Even my nightlife found me at the most popular nightspots, including, "The Oz," an exclusive private nightclub. Yes, on the outside it looked as though I had "everything under control," but it was all the illusion of control. Deep down inside, I knew that I could not sustain the slowly deteriorating facade.

The before-picture looked like this: A beautiful wife and two children, a four-bedroom, three-bathroom home furnished with expensive décor, four cars (two of which were Mercedes-Benz). Career-wise things looked promising; I was a licensed real estate broker, and co-owner of a real estate firm along with my business partner Johnny Rodgers, a 1972 Heisman Trophy Winner, who, at that time, was playing for the San Diego Chargers. I had all of this at the age of 27.

While grinding hard to move up the success ladder, I had replaced the once a week "speed" habit with a $100 a day cocaine habit. Sadly, the "I had everything under control" lie was still holding fast. Professionally I managed to develop many reputable business associates, and I'd also acquired a substantial clientele, which was steadily growing. The real estate office I managed was averaging over $1 million in active listing inventory. Johnny Rodgers and I were negotiating with a major financial corporation to put together a real estate franchising package, which, if successful, would result in our company becoming a national real estate brand.

The Fateful Introduction

Some get introduced to drugs when their life is spiraling downward, and they are looking for something to numb the pain. For others, it happens less dramatically, at a party, or by a coworker, friend, or spouse. My introduction to the cocaine world took place in the professional business community; high-powered attorneys, corporate executives, and professional athletes were among my drug-abusing clique. My point is that the problem of addiction in America is not limited to a socioeconomic class. Drug abuse is just as prevalent in our corporate and professional sectors as it is in our ghettos and lower-income communities.

This drug called cocaine is no respecter of persons. Demographic factors such as age, race, gender, or socioeconomic status do not exempt a person from potentially becoming a drug addict. I have concluded that no matter how strong you are or how strong you think you are if given the chance drugs will categorically destroy every area of your life. I don't know a single person that has played this deadly game and won. Drugs will, if given enough time, totally consume your life; every waking moment will be devoted to maintaining your habit.

In my opinion, few things can compare to the devastating effect a cocaine habit can have on a person's life. I have seen drugs take a person that was once popular, outgoing, and cheerful, and turn them into a seemingly hopeless recluse. Cocaine literally takes control of a person's entire personality. This change comes about after a period of continued drug use and its effects remain for a lifetime.

As I explained earlier, my first time was in the kitchen of a friend's house. Do you remember where you were when you tried drugs the very first time?

Looking back on those days, it's clear to see that I was falling deeper and deeper into the web of insanity and that my denial of the obvious would eventually be my undoing. Yes, "The Toothpick Castle" I had built was beginning to crumble room by room. When getting high had become my daily routine, and smoking cocaine was fast becoming the number one priority in my life, I refused to admit that I had a serious problem. That problem was getting worse and worse, one day at a time. Most of my time was spent either smoking crack or going through the motions of getting more of it to smoke and sell. When this begins to happen, there isn't much time left for family, career or any of the other necessary requisites for daily living.

> *Drug abuse is just as prevalent in our professional sectors.*

After my preoccupation with cocaine became paramount in my life, it began to negatively impact my ability to create new business, which in turn resulted in a sharp decline in my income. This brought a double negative, in that I was consistently spending money on drugs while at the same time not generating income. It doesn't take long before this dynamic begins to cause serious cash flow problems. Before I knew it, my career had taken a backseat to my newly acquired habit. This was only the beginning of the fast-approaching end of "The Toothpick Castle" that would soon come crashing down.

——— Three ———

Home Sweet Home

The harmful effects of addiction will spread like cancer in your life. You may be able to identify with what I am about to say when you think of the words "home sweet home." Those three words can take on a whole new meaning when cocaine enters the picture. In my opinion, nothing can compare to the hurt and pain a drug "habit" can have on the family unit. As I think back on the events that led to the separation from my wife and children, it still causes pain and a sense of lingering guilt. My heart is filled with deep emotional regret for what I allowed the drugs and pure selfishness to cause me to do. If it wasn't for God in my life now, I don't know how I would've been able to live with the guilt associated with the hardships I took my wife and children through.

My wife could see that I was out of control, but she never really confronted my behavior. I would come and go at all hours of the night, weighing and packaging cocaine. She saw all the money that would go through my hands, but she seemed to just put up with me. I was blinded by greed and selfishness and never stopped to consider what I was doing to her and our children.

As you read my account of this tragedy, be mindful that this same scenario is being played out in millions of homes at this very moment. It is only by the grace of God that I can look back on my experience with drugs and share my story. Thousands will never recover from the dilemma that their addictions put them in, and I can only pray that they will surrender to God's power to set them free before it's too late.

In the earlier description of my family, home, cars, career, and business pursuits, I wanted to illustrate the power of the choice I made when I said yes to drugs rather than my hopes, dreams, and aspirations. A moment of weakness changed the course of my life. Due to the priority, I had placed on supporting my addiction, I soon found myself in serious financial trouble. Instead of waking up early and going to the office, I would sleep in until noon, having spent the night before getting high, or selling cocaine at the many clubs and discos in San Diego.

Home Sweet Home

Clearly, due to my change in lifestyle, something had to give. The "Big Lie" I kept telling myself was that "I had everything under control," but the truth was I had lost control of my life. I was too proud to admit it and too selfish to quit. As a result of getting too far behind on my house payments, we lost "home sweet home." Eventually, the sheriff had to forcibly remove me from the premises. My wife and children did not have to go through this shameful experience, because they had already gone to stay with relatives in another city. I told my wife that they would only be there temporarily, and I would get the money to make up the back payments. Needless to say, that never happened, because even though I didn't want to face it at the time, the fact was, I had a bona fide full-blown crack addiction.

The effect a crack habit can have on a family's finances is devastating. It is not unusual for a cocaine habit to consume upwards of $2,000 per week, which is a conservative estimate. I once observed a professional athlete spend $2,400 smoking crack in less than twenty-four hours. When all his money was gone, he still wanted "just one more hit." Since my number one priority had become getting high, it wasn't long before I had forsaken my wife and children for the new love in my life, cocaine. I smoked coke every single day, sometimes two or three days straight. Even after the sheriff came and put padlocks on the door to our house, I kept telling my wife that everything would be all right. She was hoping against hope that I would turn things around.

With no home and all my possessions under lock and key, I recall talking to my wife on the phone. I remember her crying when she asked me, "When will our children and I be able to come home?" Sadly, I could not give her an answer. By that

A moment of weakness changed the course of my life.

time, the drugs had me totally stagnated. All I wanted to do was get high. It pains me to even share this with the world, but maybe someone will read my story and get help before my story becomes their story.

I seemingly didn't care about my family, my home, or my career. The fact was, I still did not want to admit that I was a drug addict. The year was 1979, and since that day in the kitchen of my friend's home, my life took a downward spiral until I was smoking crack every waking day. The bottom line is that my wife and children were never able to come back home, except to gather some clothes and personal belongings. My addiction had brought shame and disgrace to my family, and I didn't have the courage to be a man, ask for help, and turn my life around. At this point, my wife should have divorced me and gone on with her life, but for some reason, she continued to hang on. The separation from my family marked the beginning of my losing battle with drugs and all that goes with that kind of lifestyle.

The Big Lies I Told Myself

I know now that I was caught up in an overpowering sense of denial that caused me to rationalize every aspect of my addiction. I soon began to believe that the reason my real estate career had failed was that the government had raised the interest rates too high. I even went as far as to refer to the year I had to close down my real estate business as the "Crash of 79." The real reason was that I had placed my habit before everything else in my life. I was even able to justify, to myself, why I abandoned my family. I reasoned that they were better off without me; thereby temporarily relieving some of the guilt I was experiencing. I kept telling everyone that I was trying to get my life back on track, but that was only part of "The Big Lie." I was now totally consumed with my addiction. Many addicts fall for "The Big Lie" that says, "I'm only hurting myself," but the truth was, my addiction had a direct impact on my relationship with my spouse, 3 children, mother, siblings, and a host of other extended family and friends. Addictions don't happen in a relational vacuum.

When you find yourself caught up in the web of drug abuse there is a profound awareness that you are wrong, but there is also an innate desire to see yourself as still being okay. No one likes to admit that they have fallen victim to a drug habit, and I was no exception. Addiction will make you believe that what you are doing is only hurting you. In essence, it takes away the guilt that comes from hurting those who love and care about you. This of course is attributed to "The Big Lie." From this point on, things went from bad to worse.

With my real estate career on hold, I started selling coke to maintain my habit. This went on for a while until I became my own best customer. Out of sheer desperation, I decided to go back into the U.S. Navy. This time, I would be taking something with me, a two-year crack addiction.

Before leaving for the Navy, I was living in an oceanfront condominium in Imperial Beach. My wife and children were still at her sister's house. I was selling cocaine full time and consistently on the move. My bodyweight was low, and my health poor. I remember having a terrible cold. After being up for five days straight, I finally fell into a deep sleep. It was the day before the 1980 presidential election. Believe it or not, I slept for thirty-five hours, waking only once to use the restroom. I woke in the middle of the night the day after the election. I thought to myself, "I'm probably the only person in America that doesn't know who the President of the United States is." I had completely slept through Election Day.

I had placed my habit before everything else in my life.

My image had changed from businessman to crack head. I had become a different person, sleeping all day and running the streets all hours of the night. I was running games on people to get money for drugs. I could see what I had become, and I hated it. I hated the daylight because it reminded me of what I had become, so I would lose myself in the night. It had taken just over a year for me to become a full-blown addict, lose my home, forsake my family, and lose my self-respect. The sad part of it all was I never really tried to turn the madness around, even my decision to go back into the Navy was out of desperation. Yes, it was goodbye to "home sweet home."

—— *Four* ——

The Second Time Around

FOR THE PAST TWO years, I had been feeding an acute cocaine habit. In the early years of "freebasing" cocaine during the mid-1970s, the cocaine was taken through a chemical process using ether. When done properly the end result would be a very potent and highly addictive residue. I, of course, was very familiar with this process, because I was one of the few at that time who knew how to prepare it properly. I had totally given myself over to my addiction.

I have witnessed a person go without sleep for as many as eight days straight while freebasing cocaine. I personally have gone without sleep for five days, before literally passing out from sheer fatigue. You might ask what causes a person to abuse their minds and bodies like this? The answer is a complex one, but when I look back, the word "powerless" comes to mind. Cocaine seems to cause a person to become totally engrossed with self-gratification. It also causes what I characterized as the "Dr. Jekyll and Mr. Hyde effect," meaning, I have observed a person make a complete personality change, after just one hit of crack.

For many, taking just one hit of crack produces an insatiable desire for "just one more," even after they have consumed incredible amounts of it. I have also seen this drug cause some of the strangest behaviors you can imagine. In the early days of freebasing cocaine, the experiences were limited to relatively few, due to the complicated method of producing the freebase paste for smoking. This generated a mystique and a curiosity about freebasing cocaine that I believe is still the driving force causing so many to say, "I'm only going to try it just once," which is one of the seven "Big Lies."

That First Hit

So what is it that makes a person keep smoking cocaine even after they are high? Many abusers will report that there is a distinct original sensation that results from the first hit of crack cocaine. A future "hit" will not give them that original effect, so they keep smoking to try and match the first hit. This is the basis for my belief that 90% of crack cocaine addiction is mental. To further substantiate this premise, I believe that the reason other areas of a person's life become secondary is due to the constant preoccupation or fantasizing about the original sensation of that first hit. Many crack users will state that there is nothing like that first hit.

My decision to re-enter the Navy was out of desperation. I had lost my family, my home, and my career. I had come face-to-face with the consequences of my addiction. My back was against the proverbial wall, which forced me to take this action. Needless to say, there is no overnight cure for the problem of addiction, and I was not to be an exception to this rule. This second time around would be a direct contrast to my first time in the Navy. During my first enlistment, I was considered by many to be a model Sailor. I advanced in rank at a very quick pace and attended the best Navy schools, after which I was appointed as the advisor to the Commanding Officer in the area of The Human Goals Program. My secondary classification was as an Equal Opportunity Program Specialist (EOPS-9215), responsible for implementing the Navy Equal Opportunity Program. I was also very active in the Navy Sports Program and considered to be one of the very best athletes in the 11th Naval District. Winning would be a good word to describe my first time around in the Navy.

Now, add one cocaine habit, and let's see what happens this second time around. On the surface I tried to make myself believe that re-entering the Navy was an attempt to get my life back on track; that of course was part of "The Big Lie." Before re-enlisting, I had no job, no money, no family, and no place to call my own. What I did have was a well-seasoned drug addiction that would make all the difference in the world, concerning what kind of person was showing up for duty.

Fit for Duty?

To this day, I don't know how I passed the Re-enlistment Physical, especially because I had drugs in my system when I gave blood and urine samples. I was at least 20 pounds underweight when I stood on the scale. I was stunned when they informed me that I was considered, "fit for duty." My re-enlistment was approved, and I was given orders to report for duty in Alameda, California.

"Naval Air Station Alameda, California" were the words on the sign at the main gate. After being directed by the Personnel Office, I proceeded to "report for duty." Following a careful look at my orders, I was informed that I was one day late checking in. I explained to them that I had misread my orders. The truth was, instead of coming directly to the Naval Air Station when I arrived in Oakland, I stopped at a friend's house in East Oakland. One thing led to another and I started smoking cocaine and didn't want to stop for any reason, even at the risk of being Absent Without Leave (AWOL). I managed to talk my way out of trouble.

You see, for the last three years, I had become accustomed to coming and going as I pleased. I had a great deal of trouble adjusting to structure and discipline. In the beginning, I was able to mask my addiction with various excuses, but as the weeks went by my chronic tardiness became more and more obvious. My uniform appearance began to fall, my productivity on the job was woefully lacking, and the reason was simple; I wasn't getting the proper rest. When I got off work, usually I would start getting high and stay up all night smoking crack and drinking gin, sometimes staying up three days at a time. On many occasions, I literally fell asleep while typing or sitting at my desk. My physical appearance was beginning to deteriorate. I was losing weight and getting dark circles around my eyes. Things went from bad to worse, and I got to the point where I didn't even bother coming to work at all.

> *My decision to re-enter the Navy was out of desperation.*

I was constantly being written up for disciplinary infractions, and being counseled by my superiors. Initially, they thought I only had a drinking problem and sent me to the Naval Hospital in Oak Knoll, California, for an evaluation by a team of behavioral specialists. I was able to convince them that I was not an alcoholic. The truth is drug addicts are very convincing when it comes to talking their way out of trouble. I had dodged another bullet, but my so-called "luck" would soon run out.

AWOL...Deserter...Stockade

It wasn't long before I was under the gun again, only this time when I returned I decided that I would seek professional help for my drug problem. I was considered absent without leave (AWOL) for the past eight days. When I returned to the base, I went straight to the Personnel Office. Even as I walked in, they had begun to prepare papers declaring me a "Deserter." I remember approaching the Executive Officer to confide in him about my problem with drugs. What happened next would later shock even the most conservative military legal minds. Instead of getting help I was immediately taken to the medical dispensary and ordered to give blood and urine samples. I was also told that if I didn't give the sample voluntarily, they would be taken by force.

The test results indicated that I had cocaine in my system. I was immediately charged with possession of cocaine and ordered to stand trial by a Military Courts-Martial. A few weeks later, I was found guilty of possession of cocaine because it was in my bloodstream, and I was sentenced to 15 days in the Military Stockade, at Treasure Island in San Francisco, California. Not surprisingly, I was reduced from the rank of E-5 to the rank of E-2.

In less than eighteen months, I managed to destroy my military record by receiving a Special Courts-Martial judgment, all in the name of cocaine. Despite that ordeal, I still refused to come to grips with the fact that my cocaine habit had changed me. Keith, a friend of mine, put it best when he said, "Drugs don't make you somebody; they

Drugs don't make you somebody; they will make you somebody else.

will make you somebody else." I had become that somebody else. Next stop, the streets of East Oakland, California.

Five

Hustling

WEBSTER'S DICTIONARY GIVES THE following definition for the word *hustling*: "To obtain money aggressively or immorally." We will use that as our working definition.

After being discharged from the Navy for refusing treatment for my drug problem, I found myself with a habit and no job. So, I had two choices, I could either quit using drugs and get a job or continue using drugs and hustle for a living. I chose the latter, and my hustling days began.

In the early days of my hustling, I had little to no raw "street knowledge," and was often taken advantage of by those with more "game" than me. Without a doubt, the drug game breeds some of the most scandalous and violent behavior you can imagine, but I soon learned the ropes. My days and nights were spent smoking, buying, and selling cocaine. Having abandoned the idea of change, I became a willing member of the world of drugs and the immoral lifestyle that comes with it. I no longer wore three-piece suits every day because I had traded them for Levi's, T-shirts, and tennis shoes. I did not need a car because if I had cocaine, I had transportation. People were glad to drive me back and forth to pick up more inventory because when they were with me, they would always have crack to smoke.

It wasn't long before I had gained a reputation for always having the best crack. I made it a point to learn all I could about the drug called cocaine. I knew the melting point of cocaine, which was a test used to determine the purity of the coke. When it came to cooking cocaine, I was considered one of the best in East Oakland. I say this not to boast, but to illustrate how in just a few months I had become a completely different person. I had become a hustler. Not a badge of honor, but clear evidence of how sick and depraved my mind had become. In my opinion, you can't get much lower than a hustler. When getting high becomes your number one priority you soon become a slave to your habit. The world of hustling is one of constantly trying to "get over" on somebody by lying, cheating, deceiving, and doing whatever it takes to get what you want.

The Game

The hustling game is governed by a set of rules based on your ability to make something out of nothing. The hustler gets their greatest satisfaction when they can start a day with bus fare and their word, and before the sun goes down, they have a pocket full of money and all of the crack they can smoke. Hustling is about "Trying to make a dollar out of fifteen cents."

Communication lines are unseen by the unsuspecting public, and even by most in law enforcement. Many of the signs and symbols in the drug trafficking arena go unnoticed by the average citizen. For example, if you were driving down the street and saw a person standing on the corner, and when you made eye contact with that person, they raised their brow. You might not think much of it, but if you were looking for drugs the raised eyebrow could be a sign that the person either had drugs or knew where to get them.

Interpersonal relationships are based on what you have to offer the other guy, and of course what they have or can do for you. The golden rule of the streets is, "He or she who has the drugs makes the rules." The motto on the street is, "Be good to the game and the game will be good to you," or what's known as, "Honor among thieves!"

Many of my days were spent running in and out of crack houses, cooking, smoking, and selling crack rocks. My image as a businessman had long faded and was replaced with a reputation of always having "rocks" for sale. I was so caught up in the game that I seldom even thought about my wife and children. I tried to stay high as much as I could so that I didn't have to deal with the reality of abandoning my family. I kept believing "The Big Lie" that my family was better off without me. I was preoccupied with ways to figure out how to sell more rocks.

I Created a Monster

I had a basic understanding of concepts relating to marketing products and services so I came up with an idea that literally revolutionized how crack was sold in East Oakland and beyond. I remember it was in 1981, and at that time selling crack had just come on the scene. In those days when a person wanted to buy some rocks, they would go to a crack house in East Oakland known as the "dirt road." I remember going there a few times to buy rocks. There were always a few people sitting around smoking crack or waiting for them to cook up more rocks to sell. When a person entered, they would see a guy sitting at a table with a plate full of huge cocaine rocks. Each customer would walk up to the table, and the server would ask them how much money they wanted to spend. The server would break off what he thought was worth the amount of money being spent. When

I observed how they were doing business, I thought to myself, "This is a crude method of doing business." There was no agreed-upon standard for determining the amount of crack a person wanted to purchase. It was a very subjective way of distributing their product.

One day, while at a liquor store in West Oakland, I noticed a person buying a package of small plastic bags typically used for packing $5 bags of marijuana, and that gave me an idea. I bought a package of these clear plastic bags home with me, and after adding some "cut" and baking soda to a sixteenth ounce of cocaine, I added water, melted it down, and formed it into one huge, solid crack rock. I divided it into 12 equal parts called "doves," then I placed one dove rock in each bag and charged $20 or a "dove" for each one. To make a long story short, this method of selling rocks is how I revolutionized the rock selling business in East Oakland and beyond. It simplified what had been a crude and complex method of selling crack to the masses. For every $150, a dealer could make a profit of $170, once you factor in the "cut" added when purchasing powder cocaine.

" We came up with an idea that revolutionized how crack was sold. "

A monster had been created and that "monster" is still destroying lives until this very day. The demand for rock cocaine was so high; it wasn't long before the pressure of the game began to take its toll on me. I would be up-selling and using crack three or four days straight without sleep and having little or nothing to eat. I had to drink gin constantly to offset the "jitters" I got from smoking crack. I was always known for having a bottle of gin in my back pocket.

I can remember the early days of selling doves rocks on A Street, between 98th and 100th Avenue in East Oakland. Things were really busy on Friday nights, so busy that we would position ourselves in the middle of the block, and customers would drive up and we would serve them while still in their cars. We would go from left to right serving cars coming from both directions. This went on way into the night. The police didn't even bother to come down that street because once they turned the corner, we would run into the house until they left, then crank it back up until the next time.

98th & A Street in East Oakland, CA, where I spent many days and nights selling crack cocaine from 1982 - 1985.

The Pressure Is Suffocating

Even the cat and mouse game began to take its toll on me after a while. It seemed like every time I looked around, I would see the police. In my mind, I thought that they were always watching me, which caused me to be paranoid, and had me constantly looking over my shoulder. My greatest fear was getting busted, getting taken to jail, and not being able to get high. It was a sad state of affairs, but it was what it was. The emotional pressure that goes along with hustling was at times unbearable. The stress soon took its toll on my mind and body. This stress combined with the inner guilt caused me to be in a constant state of uneasiness. My nerves were shattered, my hair began to fall out in patches, and my stomach always burned.

> *He or she who has the drugs makes the rules.*

Between highs, I would experience moments of deep depression, even shedding tears of despair on many occasions. I couldn't deny the guilt deep down inside, but I didn't have the will or the inner strength to turn my life around. The truth is I was trying to fill the void in my life with the wrong things. As you can see, drugs had made me somebody else. It was hard to believe that only a few years earlier, I was a business owner moving up the ladder of success. I had become a shell of the man I once was, a hustler, selling drugs, and destroying lives. Yes, hustling and making money can be summed up in an old quote, which says, "A fool and his money are soon parted." There are many times when thousands of dollars would pass through my hands and when the day was over, I was flat broke, but by the same token, I can remember starting a day with no money and within a few hours I had over $1,000. Inconsistency marks the finances of a drug dealer. One thing is certain; the future of most dope dealers is jail, institutions, or death.

I have known many so-called, big-time, dope dealers and cannot think of one who has avoided at least one of the above consequences.

There is and has always been something fundamentally wrong with trying to get something for nothing. The hustling arena is an invisible network to most of society, but in the "hood" it is an everyday fact of life. For the most part, the rest of society is oblivious to the inner workings of the drug world. As I said before, there are many signs and symbols that are only recognizable to those directly involved in the drug trafficking arena.

When selling drugs became my reputation, brand, and only purpose in life, it seemed that no matter where I went in Oakland, I would be approached for crack. In stores, walking the streets, or riding in a car, if someone needed drugs, they knew that if I didn't have it, I knew where to get it. Which leads me to the saddest part about the world of hustling, the victim.

The hustling arena is an invisible network to most of society.

For the hustler to survive, he must take advantage of the weaknesses of others. Often the victim is a mother on welfare with small children to feed. When it comes to choosing between buying food and buying drugs, the drugs usually won out. Most mothers that are hooked on crack and are on welfare will usually spend their entire check on crack, having little or nothing left for food. I can remember once taking the last of a mother's food stamps in exchange for some crack, all while her children looked on.

When I think back on those days, I have deep shame and regret for the things I did which caused children to go without. I knew if that mother didn't get her drugs from me, she would get it from somebody else. No matter how I rationalized it, I couldn't shake the guilt associated with my behavior. I realize the average person cannot even imagine the real destruction drugs are causing in our society. While I was in the streets, I witnessed many things that I will never forget, all sorts of violence, many crimes, and things I can't even talk about. The truth is, it will continue to go on because people will predictably try to fill their emptiness with drugs, alcohol, and things that can only be satisfied by the love of God.

---— *Six* ———

Tweaking

N OW DON'T LOOK FOR the definition of the word "tweaking" in the dictionary. Tweaking is a word used by addicts to describe very odd behavior demonstrated by other addicts when they ingest their drug of choice. Among drug addicts, especially crack smokers; this word is all too familiar. I will give you a working definition of tweaking. It is a behavior or a mental process that takes place after ingesting just one hit of crack cocaine or methamphetamines.

Tweaking is brought on by a chemical reaction that takes place in the brain of a person that has ingested cocaine hydrochloride, the active ingredient in crack cocaine. As a direct response to this stimulus, an enzyme is released in the brain, which causes a breakdown in a person's ability to suppress fears, doubts, and uncertainties. When these negative emotions surface they cause the person to exhibit strange and bizarre behavior. This behavior is known as tweaking.

This behavioral change usually takes place after just one hit of crack or intravenous (IV) injection of speed or cocaine. I refer to it as the Dr. Jekyll and Mr. Hyde syndrome because of the dramatic change that takes place in a person's personality after using certain drugs. For example, after just one hit of the crack pipe, a normally talkative person suddenly becomes as quiet as a mouse, while, on the other hand, a person that is normally quiet will suddenly become very talkative. It is hard to say why some people behave a certain way after ingesting drugs, but one thing is clear, everybody tweaks to some degree.

The Three Stages

Let me explain why I feel it is the driving force that causes so many people to become slaves to this drug called crack cocaine. I have observed at least three distinct stages to a crack smoker's high. First, a rush occurs when the heart rate and blood flow increases. Second, a state of disorientation and depression follows; it varies in intensity and length depending on the person's metabolism and mental health. Third, a feeling of euphoria or heightened awareness ensues, coupled with a false sense of security. Once the tweak "is on" or has begun, it might take days before it finally brings its victim to a screeching halt.

Smoking cocaine is second only to IV injection when it comes to delivering the drug into the bloodstream. This jolt to the system is a tremendous strain on the vital organs of the body, which can cause a person to suffer a seizure, stroke, or even heart failure. Blackouts are common among crack smokers. Following this initial rush, a person goes through a physiological change due to the rush of blood to the brain, which alters the thinking process.

A feeling of depression and paranoia affects many crack smokers causing them to exhibit strange behaviors such as looking out the window constantly, insisting someone is coming after them or hiding for no apparent reason. There is absolutely no way to determine how a person is going to tweak until after they have taken a hit. I remember getting high with a professional basketball player who was normally talkative and lively. After just one hit off the crack pipe, he would sit in one place and not say a word the entire time we were smoking, sometimes 48 hours straight. He just sat at the table, taking hit after hit until it was all gone.

Paranoia is one of the most common characteristics of a crack smoker. Remember, smoking causes a person's fears, doubts, and uncertainties to surface in their mind. Most users have many things going on in their lives, memories that they really don't want to think about that have been suppressed into their subconscious minds. For example, many have a fear of getting busted by the police. When they smoke cocaine this fear is magnified, causing the person to think that the police are outside waiting to arrest them or that they are standing at the door about to crash through and get them.

I had a friend who I nicknamed "King Tweak" because this brother was a real tweaker. When he wasn't high, he was fun to be around, full of life, and a good conversationalist. After just one hit off the pipe, he would become a completely different person. He would go to the front door and look through the peephole for long periods, stopping only to take a quick hit and rush back to the door. This behavior persisted all night into the next day. He never told me why he was so paranoid, and I never asked him.

The Boogie Man

I can't begin to tell you to what extent this drug has control over a person's behavior. I have known people to jump through plate glass windows, take off running for no reason, jump out of moving cars, and some have even died, convinced that they were being chased by something or somebody. As Proverbs 28:1 says, "The wicked run when there is no one chasing them." They live in constant terror that the "boogie man" is trying to get them. As a person's crack habit matures, this paranoid state of mind becomes more and more obvious. They totally withdraw from society, venturing out only when necessary to do things that support their addiction. They become social outcasts, disconnected from family and friends.

The final stage of a crack-cocaine high is the false sense of euphoria that comes after the paranoia wears off. This sense of heightened awareness and self-confidence seems to overtake the initial depression and feelings of uneasiness. The craving to prolong this high is what causes so many users to do whatever they must to get more drugs. Most crack smokers' favorite saying is, "If I had just one more hit." This is of course part of "The Big Lie". The truth is when they get another hit "The Big Lie" starts all over again and may go on for days. The behavioral changes may differ, but make no mistake about it, when crack cocaine is ingested into the human body, a physiological change will occur without fail.

I have smoked cocaine with hundreds of different people, and no one tweaked the same. Each person seemed to have a distinct way of reacting to the coke. You might ask, "Dwight, how did you tweak?" Well, in the early years of smoking cocaine, I appeared to many as always having "everything under control." As the years of abuse continued, I developed a fear of being discovered or found out, which further developed into a fear of getting busted by the police. In the final stages of my addiction, I had become a nervous wreck. I was unable to sit in one place for more than five or ten minutes. My nerves got so bad that I would rub my thumb

> They become social outcasts, disconnected from family and friends.

and forefinger together until they became raw and almost bled. My hair began to fall out in patches, and I had an overwhelming sense of guilt and shame. I got to the point where I didn't need any drugs to tweak. By then, my whole life had become one big endless tweak.

One Day at a Time

Since selling rocks was how I maintained my habit, I was constantly going from house to house, selling. The demand for crack in Oakland during the early 1980s was overwhelming and extremely hard to keep up with. I was constantly on the move, buying, cooking, selling, smoking, drinking, and killing myself "one day at a time." Seeing as I was always in possession of drugs, I was constantly preoccupied with getting busted and possibly going to prison. My greatest fear was getting locked up and taken to jail. It's been said you move toward the thing you fear most, for me, that would prove to be very true.

Without a doubt, the most depressing moment for the drug addict is when they realize that they can't get high anymore. It is at this point that a cocaine habit can do the most damage. When your number one priority becomes getting just one more hit, then everything else takes a back seat to your addiction. If I'm expected at work, I'm not going to make it. If I'm wearing a nice watch, the watch will have to go. When the money's gone a person will use the next best thing to get just one more hit. Men and women have been known to trade their bodies for a hit of crack. Age is no barrier to crack addicts. I once had a customer that would come to see me on the third of every month and spend his entire social security check buying rocks. I have witnessed many older men use coke to lure young girls into giving them sexual favors.

During the seven years of my crack addiction, I could not begin to tell you the entirety of the many horrific things I witnessed. Unfortunately, the lying, stealing, cheating, fighting, and killing continue for those still caught up in that life. Homes are still being destroyed, and men and women are still going to jail, all in the name of their drug of choice. Millions of dollars are going up in smoke and into arms every hour of the day. Consuming drugs is a 24 hour a day, 365 days a year game of destruction. As the saying goes, "Around the clock the tweaking doesn't stop!"

> *Everything else takes a back seat to your addiction.*

Seven

I Could Have Been Dead

As I think back on my life when I was hanging out on the streets of Oakland, California, I can only thank God that no serious physical harm came to me. I can't deny that I did experience a tremendous amount of mental and emotional harm brought on by the constant state of stress and pressure I dealt with daily. On many occasions, I found myself in dangerous situations narrowly missing serious injury or even death.

Now, I will give some true accounts which will explain why I say, "I could have been dead, sleeping in my grave, but the Lord made ole death behave." It was about 3:30 P.M. in East Oakland, the first of the month, a day of constant activity and I had been on the go all day, nonstop. The high demand for crack kept me going from house to house, selling rocks literally 24/7.

I recall picking up a fresh package of powder cocaine, and I decided to take a break from the action to stop by a friend's apartment. With me was a guy we'll call "Joe," who was known for shooting drugs in his veins. I personally didn't like shooting my drugs, mainly because I didn't like sticking needles into my body. I preferred smoking cocaine to shooting it, but on rare occasions,

I would allow someone to shoot some powder coke into my veins. This was one of those occasions.

When we arrived, there were a few people in the small and dimly lit room, "hitting" the crack pipe and drinking alcohol. After giving Joe some powder, he fixed the cocaine in a spoon then drew about 40 cubic centimeters (cc's) into a syringe. Since it was my coke, I decided to go first. As I stuck out my arm, I began tightly squeezing my fist while holding my upper arm to make my veins easy to find. Joe tied off my arm just above the elbow, located the best vein, inserted the needle, and slowly began to empty the contents into my vein. Most IV drug users will tell you that when injecting cocaine, once the blood registers in the syringe, there is a distinct "medicinal" smell that precedes the subsequent rush from the drugs. As Joe slowly injected the coke, I watched to see how much he was giving me. When he got to about 15 ccs, I motioned for him to stop, but he didn't. I guess he thought I wanted him to shoot the whole 40 ccs into my arm. So, he ran it all in.

I suddenly experienced one of the most intense rushes I had ever had. My heart seemed like it was going to jump out of my chest, and my mind was racing out of control. As the rush subsided, I began to feel drowsy, a clear sign of a cocaine overdose. My heart could not keep up with the demand to pump blood to my vital organs, so my system began to shut down. I was dying. I tried to lie down on the floor, telling everyone that I was sleepy. Joe knew that I had overdosed. He also knew that if I went to sleep, I would never wake up again. He frantically motioned for others to help him pick

> I began to feel drowsy, a clear sign of a cocaine overdose.

me up. They began walking me around so that my blood would circulate properly. It took about 30 minutes before I could function on my own.

When the word got out that I had almost died from an overdose, many thought Joe had tried to kill me, but I was sure that was not the case. Joe and I had many dealings over the past few years, and he and I stayed "true to the game" in our dealings with one another. Yet, even this close brush with death did not bring me to my senses; I continued traveling down the road of destruction.

Master Blaster

A few months later in a hotel room on MacArthur Boulevard, in East Oakland, I was sitting on the bed smoking some rocks, drinking gin, and kickin' it with a few friends. I had been up grinding for about four days straight. Suddenly, after taking a "master blaster" off the pipe, I felt a sharp pain go up the left side of my neck and I fell back on the bed. My body went limp. I could not move any part of my body; I could not talk or move my mouth at all. The only thing I could do was move my eyes.

I was consumed with fear that I had suffered a massive stroke or something worse. Everyone was scared. They didn't know what to do. Since I could not speak, I could not tell them what was wrong with me. I lay in that state for about 30 minutes before finally regaining control of my body. I guess I had some sort of seizure that could have resulted in a stroke or even death. I had witnessed something similar happen to other addicts while using. They would temporarily pass out, only to wake up, asking if it was their turn to hit the pipe again.

When this happened, I told myself that I was going to quit smoking crack, but because the chains of habit were still wrapped tightly around my neck, my resolve only lasted for about two weeks. Soon, the craving got so strong that I went back to smoking again. You might ask, "Why did you continue to use drugs after coming so close to death?" There is no easy answer to that question, except to say it seems as though the further away in time you get from a crisis, the less of an effect it seems to have on you. So not having the will or the power within to quit smoking coke, I continued to take the risk necessary to support my habit. I could see the destruction drugs were causing in my life and the lives of others, but I refused to heed the warning signs. I had begun to buy into the lie that there was no hope for me. I had surrendered to my addiction, and I believed that I would be an addict until my dying day.

Enough Is Enough?

It didn't take long before I was back to my routine of staying up three to four days at a time, getting high and selling rocks. The human body was never designed to take that kind of abuse, and it would soon give me a serious warning that enough was enough. For about two months, I had been feeling like something was wrong in my body. The left side of my body had begun to ache constantly. My jaw would feel numb, and the numbness would radiate all the way down my left leg. The cocaine would give me temporary relief from the pain, but when the drugs wore off the ache would return with a vengeance. I thought about the warning signs of a heart attack or stroke, but I wouldn't go to the doctor to have it checked out.

Living with this level of chaos had become my norm. I had been on the go for the past few days and under a tremendous amount of stress due to basically being homeless. One morning, while getting high at a friend's house, I remember taking a hit off the pipe, and suddenly feeling an extremely sharp pain in my chest area. I let out a loud groan, clenched my chest, and held my breath. It seemed that whenever I would inhale, the pain got sharper and more intense. I thought I was having a heart attack, and the fear only made it

> I believed that I would be an addict until my dying day.

worse. Someone went and woke up my friend, and he then rushed me to Highland Hospital, near downtown Oakland. The pain in my chest was so intense that tears came to my eyes because I thought I was going to die. I could only take short breaths, which caused the muscles in my chest area to tighten even more. I yelled out in pain. At the hospital, I was rushed into the emergency room, hooked up to all types of monitoring equipment, and given an IV.

As I lay there many things went through my mind. I knew the cocaine and my destructive lifestyle had caused this to happen. When questioned about my drug use, I told the doctor I had been using cocaine for about five years. The test determined that I was suffering from acute muscle spasms in my chest area, which put pressure on my heart, causing intense pain. When my vital signs returned to normal, the nurse began disconnecting me from the machines. Just before releasing me, the attending nurse looked me in the eyes and said, "If you don't quit using cocaine, you will soon be dead."

I thought about those words for a long time, but again after a few days, it was back to business as usual, smoking and selling rocks, drinking gin, and living a reckless, irresponsible lifestyle. I just didn't have the will or the strength to overcome the control the drugs had over my life. Once again, "I could have been dead, and sleeping in my grave." Of course, I attributed it to just being lucky.

Huey P. Newton

The next incident I will share involves a person of national notoriety. I feel the necessity to give some background before going into details. The person involved was the co-founder of the Black Panther Party, Huey P. Newton. My purpose in telling this story is not to defame Huey as a person, but to illustrate how this drug called crack cocaine can bring down even the most intelligent and articulate of our society. It gives more credence to why we should continue to wage an all-out war on this evil that is dismantling our country at the very core of its moral fiber.

The day I met Huey was not particularly different than any other since I was about the business of selling rocks and smoking coke. It was the early 1980s, and I had just picked up a new package of coke. After rocking it up, I packaged up some "dove rocks" and was ready to get my grind on. While standing on the turf someone came over to let me know that Huey Newton was across the street, and he wanted to buy some rocks.

I thought to myself, "Huey Newton... 'The' Huey P. Newton?!" Since I had grown up in the decade of the sixties, I had read about the Black Panther Party. I had seen them on television with their black leather jackets, black berets, and their notoriety for carrying guns in public. I considered Huey a symbol of Black pride and a catalyst for change in our society. He was calling on us as Black people to seize the time before the time seized us.

When I walked into the room, I sensed some tension in the air. I went to the kitchen table, sat down, and took out a few dove rocks. I laid the pistol I was carrying on the table. Huey looked at the gun and asked me to let him see it. I handed it to him. After looking it over, he slid it back across the table to me. He then bought some rocks and I left. I remember walking back across the street thinking about the fact that I had just sold some rocks to Huey P. Newton.

The next time I saw Huey was about three days later when he came to the house where I was selling rocks. I came out to the car and he motioned for me to get in. I did and we drove off. As we drove through the streets of Oakland, we talked about many things. I was amazed at the level of intelligence with which he spoke. It was as though I was riding with a college professor, and I was his only student. Huey shared moments from his life, like how they organized the meal program for children. He even took me near Seminary and

> He was very proud of what he had accomplished in the community of Oakland.

MacArthur Blvd., the place where it all began. As he spoke, I sensed that he was very proud of what he had accomplished in the community of Oakland. Huey also talked about his exile in Cuba and how he was treated in a foreign country. I believe it was that experience in Cuba that really shaped his life and intensified his commitment to social change.

We rode around for about two hours, with Huey doing most of the talking. I asked a lot of questions about his life and experiences. Huey had a very subtle sense of humor with an acute ability for reasoning. To my surprise, drugs didn't even come into the conversation. When we finally got back to A Street, I jumped out of his red Mercedes-Benz and went into the house. I couldn't believe that I had actually been with Huey P. Newton.

My next visit with Huey would not be quite so pleasant. The instrument of that change would be a little white rock called crack cocaine. It was the one thing Huey and I had in common and it would be the change agent that was controlling our every waking moment. Just like my friend Keith said, "Drugs don't make you somebody; they make you somebody else."

I had been on the "turf" grinding rocks all day when Huey pulled up and asked for a $100 package of rocks. I fixed him up with a fat package and he asked me if I knew where he could smoke it. We went to a friend's house nearby. After he finished smoking the first package, he bought another. This went on for about six hours. I kept leaving to get more drugs. This routine went on into the next day, and it seemed as though he had an endless supply of $100 bills. After spending over $2,000, he started to run low on money. We decided to go out to his house in the Claremont area. On our way, we picked up a package of coke and a lady friend, and then off we went to Huey's house in the suburbs. His house was very nice and set back off the beaten path.

Things started with everybody having a good time smoking, drinking, and socializing until all the drugs were gone, and that's when attitudes began to change and tempers began to get short. We had been going up and down the stairs of Huey's spacious two-story executive home. As we were sitting down trying to figure out how we were going to get more drugs, Huey jumped up suddenly and asked, "Who has my ring?" I had no idea what he was talking about. As he continued to question us, the girl with us stood up and confessed to taking the ring. Things got intense after that, with Huey expressing his outrage over the fact that someone would come into his home and take something that belonged to him. He even accused me of having something to do with his ring being taken, but I assured him that was not the case. With threats of taking us both out and shooting us, I feared for my life, while we were at gunpoint.

After about an hour of some pretty dramatic events, for some reason, he had a sudden change of heart about what he thought about doing to us. We got in the car to return home. It was a long ride back to A Street in East Oakland, but it beat the alternative that could have played out. I can truly say that was an ordeal I will never forget. It may sound strange to some, but I am convinced that God was with me through the prayers of my mother that day.

"Lord, have mercy!"

A few days after that incident, I called my mother in Arkansas. She told me that on the very day that incident occurred, I suddenly came to her mind and a strong feeling of fear overtook her. The fear was so strong that all she could say was "Lord, have mercy!" I truly believe that my mother's plea to God is partly what kept me from being shot that day. I still don't totally understand it, but I believe my mother's intercession touched the heart of God. I thank God for His mercy, and I thank Him for my mother's prayers.

Yes, "I could have been dead and sleeping in my grave, but the Lord made ole death behave." In looking back on that experience, I can't help but wonder why I was living such a dangerous life. The truth is I thought I was just lucky, but the reality was that God's hand of mercy was on me. He knew that one day I would come to know the Truth, and the Truth would make me free.

I had a few more, less dramatic encounters with Huey, and then eventually lost touch with him. I later heard that he had been shot and killed in West Oakland. When I heard the sad news of his passing, I reflected back on the time I had spent with him. I thought about how drugs had impacted both our lives in such a devastating way. Fortunately, the young lady that accompanied us to Huey's house later experienced a spiritual conversion through Jesus Christ and went on to help many others get free from the bondage of drug addiction.

Huey was a symbol of Black pride and a catalyst for change in our society.

—— *Eight* ——

You're Under Arrest

"**Y**OU'RE UNDER ARREST," ARE the three words drug addicts and dope dealers dread hearing. When people make dealing in drugs their lifestyle, sooner or later, they are going to face jail, institutions, or death.

During the first three years of my drug-dealing days, I had an uncanny ability to avoid the police, in part because I didn't look like the typical street dealer. When stopped by the police I was able to convince them that I was a clean-cut young man, since my appearance didn't fit the stereotype of a street drug dealer. In the weeks and months that followed, my physical appearance and dress began to change dramatically. I lost twenty to thirty pounds and dressed in Levi's, tee shirts, and tennis shoes. It seemed that whenever there was a drug bust at the place I would purchase my drugs, I would miss it by minutes. Many times, I would either be just leaving, or when I arrived a bust would already be going down, so I would just keep it moving, and wait until things cooled off and come back later for my drugs.

The common characteristic among most street dealers is that they are constantly looking over their shoulder for the police or some tweaker trying to rob them. From 1982 until 1986, if someone was looking for crack cocaine in East Oakland, they could always find me grinding on A Street between 98th and 100th Avenue; that's where I felt safe using and selling drugs. I was very familiar with who belonged there and who was just passing through to pick up some rocks.

Most of the time dealers looked out for each other. For instance, when I would go into the house to cook and package some dove rocks, someone would inform me when the police (rollers) were nearby. The bottom line is that you always want to be able to see the police before they see you because if you get caught sleeping, you just might end up sitting in the back of a patrol car on your way to jail.

My Worst Nightmare

It was Denzel Washington who said, "In life, there is the moment, and then there is after the moment in which nothing is ever the same again." I was about to experience one of those game-changing moments. It was around 6 A.M. and I had been up all night smoking and selling rocks. I stepped outside for a minute when suddenly a car pulled up and I recognized it to be one of my regular customers. He called me over to the car and I got in. He asked if I had any rocks for sale. I told him, "Yes." He didn't have any money and wanted to know if he could get a dove rock on credit. I told him, "No," and proceeded to get out of the car.

As I stepped out, I noticed a car coming up fast. It was the police. Before I could take another step, the officer jumped out and said, "Freeze." My heart dropped to my feet and my mind flooded with ways to escape, but it was too late. He told me to put my hands up where he could see them. I felt him grab my hands and put them together behind my back; Then, I felt the pressure of the cold steel as he handcuffed me. He reached into my pocket and pulled out a little plastic bag containing twelve dove rocks. The next words I heard were, "You're under arrest for possession of cocaine with the intent to sell. A violation of the health and safety code 113500." He put me in the back seat of his car.

There are few feelings worse than sitting in the back seat of a patrol car waiting to be taken to jail. My luck had finally run out. Things would never be the same for me again on the streets of Oakland. As I sat in that car thinking about how the bust went down, I wondered if it was a set-up, but at the end of the day, that didn't matter. I was on my way to jail with a possession for sale case hanging over my head.

The arresting officer was a cop named Jack Lundquist, Jr., who had vowed that he would put me in prison one day. He had finally accomplished the first step in making good on his vow. When he questioned me, I kept wishing I was having a bad dream and would soon wake up safe and sound in my bed, but this was no dream. The handcuffs around my wrists were real, the officer asking me the questions was real, and the fact that I was on my way to jail was depressingly real. Yes, my worst nightmare had come true.

First, I was taken to a designated point, the "Big O Tires" store on 98th and East 14th, and transferred to a paddy wagon which would take me downtown for booking. The officer removed the handcuffs and pushed me into the van with others who had been arrested that night. I did not say a word to anyone. When someone attempted to strike up a conversation, I gave

There are few feelings worse than sitting in the back seat of a patrol car.

them a blank look and put my head down. I kept thinking back on how I could have avoided all the madness I was about to endure.

To say I was depressed would be a gross understatement. After being processed and fingerprinted, I was taken to a cell with about fifteen other men having their own version of a bad day. The cell had only two metal benches and one filthy toilet, so I found a spot in the corner, lay down on the floor, and went to sleep.

Wait...What?

The following morning, I went before the judge, and for some unknown reason, I was released with all charges dropped. I don't know why they cut me loose, and I never asked, but I was happy, happy, happy! Less than three hours after being released I was back on A Street grinding rocks, but ever-present in my mind was that fear of getting busted and going back to jail, again.

As I look back on my first brush with the law, it was one of the most depressing experiences I had ever had. I was handcuffed, placed in a police car, stuffed into a paddy wagon, fingerprinted, stripped naked, subjected to a degrading body inspection, thrown into an overcrowded cell, fed jail food, and treated like a caged animal. The experience is something you can't imagine in your wildest nightmares, but that's the chance you take when you get caught up in the drug game.

After getting busted things were never the same again because I became paranoid. When I would get high the cocaine intensified my fears to the point that I was over cautious and thought the police were always watching me. Even though the charges were dropped, I knew the district attorney could refile charges up to one year from the day I was arrested, so I was trying to be extra careful.

Obsessed Meets Harrassed

Since the police now knew me as a narcotics offender, I was frequently stopped, searched, questioned, and on most occasions allowed to go. I was constantly harassed by Officer Lundquist because he still wanted to make good on his promise to send me to prison. If he saw me go into a house he would stop out front, and with his loudspeaker would say things like, "So this is where the new drug house is," and he would declare, "I'm going to get you, Dwight." It got to the point that whenever I saw him coming down the street, I would hide or run into the house. I literally felt like a fugitive constantly on the run.

Then it happened again. It was about 6:00 A.M. and I had just copped a fresh package of powder cocaine. I cooked up some rocks and packaged up some doves to sell. After taking a couple hits, I decided to go home. For some reason, I decided to leave my money with a friend. When I left, I had about twelve $20 rocks in my pocket.

A couple buddies and I started walking to the house on A Street, and as we got to the front gate a car drove up. The driver called me over and he showed me a diamond ring that he wanted to trade for some rocks. I told him I only wanted cash, and as I was about to walk away, I noticed a car coming up on me fast. I turned, looked, and it was Officer Lundquist, the same cop that had been harassing me. He skidded his brakes and leaped out of his patrol car. I broke for the front door of the house, which is usually always unlocked, but on this occasion, it was locked. I started banging on it, hoping someone would come to open it, but by this time Lundquist was out of his car and heading towards me. He commanded me to stop and come down the stairs. Before turning, I managed to get some of the packets out of my pocket and sling them onto the porch. As I was coming towards him, I asked him why he was harassing me. He kept motioning for me to come down the stairs. After handcuffing me, he walked up to the porch and picked up my drugs. When he turned around, he said, "You're under arrest for possession of cocaine for sale." He then escorted me to the car. I thought to myself, "Here I go again."

As Officer Lundquist was filling out the arrest report, I was sure they weren't going to drop the charges this time. I'm going to have to fight this case in court." I sat in the back of the patrol car watching people through the window thinking what I wouldn't give to trade places with any one of them. I soon fell fast asleep only to be awakened when we got to the county jail in downtown Oakland.

Even though I had been through this routine before, I was depressed by the ordeal. There is something about being locked up that you never really get used to. Since I had been without sleep for nearly forty-eight hours, after being booked, I went to sleep and would only wake up to eat. This was my routine for about three days because I was arrested on Friday and could not see a judge until Monday morning.

Blessed Recognizance

When Monday finally arrived, I was able to speak to a public defender. He said he would ask the judge to let me out on my own recognizance, which meant I would agree to report for all court appearances. As I stood before the judge, he read the charges, and to my surprise, I was only charged with possession of cocaine. The possession for sale part of the charge was dropped, likely because it was more difficult to prove I had the intent to sell. After hearing the charges, I was advised to plead not guilty, and that's just what I did. I was later released on my own recognizance; again, I was happy, happy, happy!

You might ask why, with a felony case hanging over my head and knowing that if I got busted again it would insure my conviction in the case I was fighting, didn't I just get my act together and stop smoking and selling drugs? The truth is, the chains of habit were still wrapped tightly around my neck and I didn't even have a mind to want to quit using and selling.

There is something about being locked up that you never really get used to.

I was willing to risk my freedom for my addiction. It's as simple as that. I didn't have the inner power it took to quit using cocaine, so I simply returned to getting high, drinking, and selling rocks.

Since I had become a known drug dealer by the neighborhood police, I had to become less visible. I began to limit my dealing activities to certain houses, only going out to cop more drugs and making it straight back to the house. This went on for about a year. When things got shaky for me, and I didn't have any product to sell, I went to work in one of my supplier's crack houses on 65th Avenue. I made $150 a day plus all I wanted to smoke. I would usually take my pay in drugs and this would be a start-up package to get me up and selling again.

Over time, trust began to develop between my supplier and I. We were the only ones who knew the combination to his safe where he kept the drugs and money. One day when he asked me to run the house for him, I told him, "Yes." This involved handling the weighing of the powder cocaine and the counting and handling of the money. When a customer would come for a package, a "server" would bring the money to me and I would make up the package and send it down. This went on all night and into the next day.

At about 6:00 P.M. I decided to go home to change clothes and check on the guy that was selling rocks for me over on A Street. With all the drugs and money locked in a safe, I left the house with a couple of friends. As we were driving along, I noticed the guy who was selling drugs for me heading towards the house we had just left. I knew he was bringing me some money, so I told the guy that I was riding with to turn around and go back to the house.

Boom! Crash!

When we pulled up to the house, there were a lot of people coming and going, but I didn't give it much thought. I met my friend in the driveway and told him to come into the house so that we could take care of business. As we were walking in, he said something about a helicopter overhead, I ignored the comment and said, "Come on man." The door had been opened, so we swiftly entered the house.

We stopped in the front room and began to talk, and it had only been about thirty seconds later when I heard a loud BOOM! CRASH! I turned and looked, thinking someone had been shot because we had several guns in the house. I then heard a lot of noise at the front door. It was a narcotics raid; police were everywhere. The next thing I knew, I was told to get down on the floor or I'd be blown away. I quickly did as I was told, not bothering to look up to see who was doing the talking. I was told to put my hands behind my back and was immediately handcuffed.

As I lay there on the floor, I could hear the police yelling and women screaming throughout the house. The police were cursing and yelling, and they called us everything but a child of God. I was then turned over and told to sit against the wall along with the others. We were all brought into one room. I counted fourteen people and about twenty heavily armed policemen with shotguns, pistols, rifles, and wearing bulletproof vests. They were well prepared for any situation that might arise.

After about thirty minutes we were lined up, led out, and escorted to a police van. I noticed a crowd of people standing around watching as we were put into the vans headed for jail. They put men and women in the same vehicles. We laughed and joked all the way, but beneath the laughter was the ever-present reality that we were on our way to jail, nothing could overshadow that reality.

Once we arrived at the police station, we were taken to special holding cells in the narcotics division. As we were escorted to our cells, we passed the evidence on the table: drugs, money, guns, and other miscellaneous items. There is a feeling that you never get used to when you enter a jail cell and the door closes behind you; a profound feeling of emptiness, helplessness, and utter despair overpow-

I was told to get down on the floor or I'd be blown away.

ers you. This time was no exception. As I sat down, I thought to myself, "Well this is it," because I already have two drug-related arrests against me and now a third. After being taken to the main jail, we were put in a dorm-like room for the night.

The next morning, they woke us up early to eat and wait to be arraigned. They kept everyone who was seeing the judge moving from tank to tank. When we got there, we ran into an old friend I knew from the streets. When we asked him what he was being charged with, he looked at us with a distant stare and said, 1-8-7, which is code for murder. I later learned that he was being charged for killing a motel owner on MacArthur Boulevard. He didn't seem to be letting it affect him, but I knew beneath the surface he was very concerned.

That Happy Feeling

After a couple of hours, they began to call us in, one-by-one. I was very nervous because of the case I already had pending. When my turn came, I went out and to my surprise, they told me that I was not being charged because it wasn't my house and they couldn't prove that the drugs belonged to me. Yes, you guessed it; I was happy, happy, happy! Upon getting released, some of us went back to the house. When we arrived, a couple of people were just sitting around. The place was a total mess. They had literally turned the house upside down looking for drugs. It looked as if a bomb had gone off, but two days later it was back to business as usual, a 24/7 operation, pumping cocaine.

My first order of business was getting some drugs. Oftentimes when a drug dealer gets out of jail, he can usually go to his main source to get a startup package on credit. I went to my main connection and he gave me a package of powder, and I was off to the races again.

My nerves were bad, my health was failing, and I had no peace of mind.

My many run-ins with the police were beginning to get to me. I was constantly looking over my shoulder. I was frequently stopped, searched, and put in the car for a warrant check. The computer would always reflect the fact that I was a narcotics offender. My nerves were bad, my health was failing, and most of all I had no peace of mind, but I was caught up in a web of insanity and could not get free. I had truly become another person. I was constantly on the go, taking chances, risking death, and my freedom, all in the name of cocaine.

I remember it was about 3:00 A.M. and I had been hustling all day and into the night. I had started the day with nothing but bus fare from West to East Oakland and managed to make $700 in cash and had about $1,000 in inventory on me. I was going to make one last stop to sell a package and then go home. I told my friend to stop at a phone booth, and for some reason, he passed two phone booths before stopping. I got out and made a call. I wanted to make sure the person who requested the drugs was there with the money. While making the call, I remember thinking and feeling that something was wrong, but I didn't give it much thought.

"If Dwight is around..."

We headed for the house, and just as we made the last turn, I noticed a "roller" coming from the other direction. My heart began to beat fast as he turned down the same street behind us. Just as we pulled up into the driveway of the house, the police turned his light on behind us. My heart dropped to my stomach, and my mind was racing.

My first thought was to get the drugs out of my pockets. I put them under the seat figuring I would be taken out of the car and searched. The officer jumped out of his car and told us to raise our hands where he could see them. Next, he ordered us to get out of the car and directed us to put our hands on the patrol car, at which time we were thoroughly searched. Just as he was about to let us go, a backup unit pulled up, and my old friend, Officer Lundquist, jumped out of his car. I thought to myself, "Oh no!" He walked over to the car and looked me in the eye. He then asked the other officer if he found anything. The officer responded, "No." Then Officer Lundquist made the comment, "If Dwight is around, drugs are around." He then casually walked back to our car and shined his flashlight through the window, where he saw drugs on the floorboard on the passenger's side. Suddenly, I saw him moving quickly, opening the door on the passenger side. I looked and thought here we go again. He motioned for his partner to handcuff us and put us in the car.

Badge of Officer Jack Lundquist, Jr., the officer who arrested me three times between 1983 and 1985.

As they put us into the back seat of the patrol car, I noticed the look of disgust on my friend's face, but he couldn't have felt any worse than me. I could see people begin to look out the window at us. They would have to get their drugs from someone else tonight because all my drugs were now in a police evidence bag, not to be seen again until they would be presented as exhibit "A" in a court of law. Yes, just when it seemed like I was getting ahead in the game, the bottom dropped out of my world again.

We were quickly taken to the parking lot of a "Big O Tires" store. As we sat in the back seat, I could feel my handcuffs beginning to pinch badly. I informed the officer and he got out and loosened the cuffs. I thought that was nice of him. I wished he would have taken them off and let me go home, but that was just a silly fantasy; I was on my way to jail, again.

When I sat back down, I looked up and saw my sister Brenda walking by with some friends. I know she hated to see her brother in a police car. As she walked by, I thought to myself, "How could I have ever let my life get so out of control?"

After getting booked, I entered an all too familiar holding cell and fell sound asleep. Whenever I went to jail, I would sleep as much as possible, hoping I would have a good dream before waking up to the nightmare of being locked up. The next morning I went before the judge, and because of my previous arrests on the same charges he would not release me on my own recognizance, so unless I

How could I have ever let my life get so out of control?

posted bail I would have to remain in custody, and would be transferred to the county jail at Santa Rita Rehabilitation Center.

My bail was only $2,000, which meant I had to post $200. Since all my money was being held as evidence, I had to depend on someone on the outside to put up my bail. I sat in jail eight days before my girlfriend's mother finally posted bail for me. The term "out of sight, out of mind" is appropriate here.

After this last bust, there was no doubt that I would have to spend some time in jail. I just hoped I wouldn't be sent to the state penitentiary. If this case went to trial, I was looking at a maximum of five years on each count. Yes, things were looking bad for the home team. Next stop, the criminal justice system.

---- *Nine* ----

The Criminal Justice System

S TANDING ON THE CORNER of 98th and East 14th Street in Oakland, waiting for the number 83 downtown bus, I was on my way to an appointment to see my public defender who I will call "Mr. Smith." I knew that the news concerning my case would not be good, since I had just added another possession charge to it. Before the second incident, I had an outside chance of beating the case if it went to trial, but there was no chance of that now. He informed me that the district attorney was going to consolidate the two possession cases, which meant my chances of being found not guilty by a jury were very slim.

I was facing a "let's make a deal" moment or what is commonly known as the "plea bargain," with the district attorney. Before my last bust, the district attorney had offered me one year in the county jail, three years' probation, and a guarantee of no state penitentiary time. This time I was offered six to nine months in county jail, two and a half years' probation, and a guarantee of no state penitentiary time. My attorney advised me to go for it. I agreed to it because I was looking at three to five years in the state penitentiary if found guilty in a trial by jury. In return for the district attorney's offer, I had to plead guilty to one count of cocaine possession, which is a felony.

Mr. Smith informed me that I was eligible for the "Work Furlough Program," on the condition that I found a full-time job before coming back to court. I managed to find a part-time job through a friend I had grown up in Redlands, California. Her name was Tony Nash. When I returned to court the judge ordered me to report to the work furlough department. Just as my attorney had said, they informed me that I would have to get a full-time job. I soon found a job at Burger King in the Eastmont Mall in East Oakland.

I was due back in court on November 15th, and of course, I had been smoking and selling rocks up to that very day. On the 13th, I had managed to buy a big package of powder cocaine, which meant I wouldn't get any sleep before my court date. The day I was to be in court, I set up a $1,200 deal and told my customers that I would be out of court no later than noon. My lawyer told me that he was going to see if he could get the judge to refer me back to the work furlough program because I had obtained a full-time job.

Even though I had been up getting high all night, I knew I couldn't miss my court date. Somehow, that morning I managed to pull myself away from the crack pipe long enough to get showered and dressed. Even while taking that last hit off the pipe, I was thinking of how I could somehow get out of going to court that morning. To be honest, the control of the crack almost overpowered my sense of reason; thank God it didn't prevail.

> *The control of the crack almost overpowered my sense of reason.*

As I was leaving the house, I let everyone know that I would be back right after court, because I had some business to handle.

I knew I was going to be late for court, and that only added to the anxiety and fear that began to grip my mind. When I arrived at the courthouse, my lawyer rushed me into the hallway and asked where I had been. My case had already been called. I told him that I had done my best to get there on time. We returned to the courtroom and my attorney let the court clerk know that I was present.

The People vs. Dwight Pledger

As I sat waiting to be called, I was not thinking about what I was going to say to the judge, but about what I was going to do after I got out of court. "Finally, I heard the clerk say, "The People of California vs. Dwight Pledger." I stood with my attorney and the judge asked me to step forward. I tried my best to look alert and focused. He then asked me why I was late. I told him that I thought I had arrived at the correct time. At this point, I began to get a little nervous but tried to maintain my composure.

The judge then asked me why I hadn't reported to the work furlough program as he had previously instructed. I told him that I had gone to the work furlough program and was told to get a full-time job. My lawyer then informed the judge that I now had a full-time job and would like to be referred to the work furlough program again. The judge told us that the clerk at the work furlough program said she didn't have any record of me reporting to her. The judge then looked straight at me and said, "I am now going to pass sentence on this case." My mouth fell open and I had a sick feeling in my stomach. He then said, "Having entered a plea of guilty to the charge of possession of cocaine, I sentence you to three years, of which, six months is to be served in the county jail, after which you will serve a two and half year probation term." Mr. Smith then requested that the judge postpone carrying out the sentence until we could prove that I had reported to the work furlough program.

In desperation, I told the judge that I had given my papers to the lady at work furlough. The judge paused for a minute, then said, "I'm sorry, you are remanded into custody to begin serving your sentence." He then instructed the bailiff to take me away. I turned to my lawyer and said, "But I did report." He assured me that he would try to get the judge to change his mind. I couldn't believe what was happening to me. After being handcuffed, I was escorted out of the courtroom.

As I sat in the holding cell, I thought about the day I had planned and the people I was supposed to be meeting after court. I also realized that the judge was not likely to modify his decision. I stretched out on the hard, cold, metal bench and tried to go to sleep while waiting to be transferred to Santa Rita Rehabilitation Center in Pleasanton, California. I don't know how long I was asleep before being awakened by a loud voice calling out my name, "Pledger! Dwight Pledger!" The guard stopped at my cell, checked my wristband, opened the door, and escorted me to the sheriff's bus bound for Santa Rita. After getting on the bus, I noticed a few familiar faces I had seen on the streets. I made eye contact with them, and then found a seat in the back of the bus.

> *I had danced to the music, and it was now time to pay the piper.*

After sitting down, I took a deep breath and one last look at the city of Oakland. I also thought about the mess I had made of my life. I had danced to the music, and it was now time to pay the piper. I had finally hit rock bottom. I had let down and disappointed so many people, my mother, wife, three children, and many others who were hoping that I would turn my life around.

The Break I Needed

Once a relatively successful businessman headed to the top, I was now nothing more than a convicted felon and addict with nothing more to look forward to than a six-month stretch in the county jail. Beneath it all, I knew that this break in the action was just what I needed. The plain truth was I had grown tired of the life I was living; my health had gone bad; my weight was incredibly low; my mental stability was fragile, and the pressure was beginning to be unbearable. The daily abuse of my body had taken its toll. I needed to take a break.

Upon arriving at Santa Rita Rehabilitation Center, we were led to a large holding tank with several benches and a toilet. The room was cold, and everything was hard. A part of the processing procedure was an interview in which you were asked a series of questions, such as; do you have a gang affiliation? What's your sexual orientation? There were also many health and work-related questions.

After a fingerprinting session and a mug shot, I was given a set of prison clothes and shoes. I was then taken to a temporary dorm until I'd be assigned work detail. During my job interview, I mentioned that I was a skilled typist with ten years of practical experience, so I was given an interview with the fire chief. I explained a little about my past and shared with him how I was going to get my life back together upon my release from Santa Rita. I also told him that I was trying to get accepted into the work furlough program. I knew from the talk around the compound that the fire chief could pull a few strings and get a person into the program with just a phone call. I really tried to impress the chief. After meeting with him, I headed back to the dorm.

Boy...Bye!

I was fortunate enough to be put in a racially mixed dorm with private showers. The other dorms were more segregated with, all Blacks, Whites or Latinos, and were known for drug activity, fighting, and constant noise. One day, I ventured over to the fence that separated my dorm from the segregated dorms, and an inmate came up to the fence and tried to start some trouble with me. He thought I was going to climb over the fence to fight him. I looked at him like he was crazy and made my way back to my dorm.

I spent most of my time reading, watching television, and writing letters, which brought me to a conclusion about the criminal justice system; I discovered that county jails were simply rest and relaxation centers for criminals as most of the conversation was centered on figuring out how to become better at committing crimes. There was never any sense of remorse exhibited by the inmates. I knew that no one wanted to be locked up, but they seem to make the most out of a bad situation.

With that said, during confinement tempers could run short and fights could break out quickly; there was at least one fight every day. Stealing food from the chow hall was the main hustle for many of the inmates. Cigarettes were the main medium of exchange. I didn't smoke cigarettes, but I always kept a few packs on hand in case I wanted to trade them for something I needed. We were permitted to attend church services at least once a week. I tried not to miss any of the services, even though I felt very uncomfortable. I would just sit, listen, and watch the show. I was so self-centered that I never really considered receiving Jesus as my Lord and Savior while I was at Santa Rita. All that time, Jesus was standing at the door to my heart, knocking, but I wouldn't let Him in.

The Santa Ritan

After being in Santa Rita for two weeks, I was assigned to the fire station, which was considered one of the most desirable places to work. We even wore special clothes that distinguished the fire crew from the other inmates. I had only been at the fire station one week, before being called to work in the print shop and given the job as the Editor of the "Santa Ritan", which was the prison newspaper. My typing skills had definitely paid off. When I started working as editor, the paper was two months behind. Just prior to my leaving Santa Rita, it was one month ahead. The fire chief was very pleased with my work and seemed to take a liking to me. He showed his gratitude by calling his friend at the Work Furlough Program and gave me a strong recommendation for the program.

Early one Thursday morning, I thought I was dreaming when I heard my name being called, "Dwight Pledger! Dwight Pledger!" I said, "Yes, right here," then the guard said, "Get your bags packed! You're going to work furlough today." I grabbed my stuff, said good-bye to a couple of friends, and was gone. I had been looking forward to this day ever since I got here. Yes, I was happy, happy, happy!

Let me take just a minute to explain how the Work Furlough Program functions. First, to qualify for the program a person must have a job before being incarcerated. The program allows a person to go to his or her place of employment and return each day to the Work Furlough Center on 12th Street in Oakland. The work furlough concept made sense because it allowed a person the opportunity to maintain their job while paying their debt to society. It also served to facilitate the transition from incarceration back to civilian life. The sheriff's deputies run the center, monitoring the comings and goings of the inmates. Inmates are also subject to a urinalysis at any time and any place. If any drugs or alcohol are found in their system, they are immediately sent back to Santa Rita. Inmates are directed to go directly to work and then back to the center. We were not allowed to visit anyone while traveling to and from work. A sheriff's deputy dressed in plain clothes would often follow inmates to work in hopes of citing violations.

Just Less Confined

The conditions at the center were like Disneyland compared to Santa Rita. The food was great, and they gave us plenty of it. I could not think of any better way to pay my debt to society. I remember the first day I went to work and how good it felt to be back out in the public. Since my job was quite a distance from the center, I had to catch a bus. Of course, I didn't mind at all; I was just happy to get away from jail life for eight hours. Although the conditions were much better at the center, it doesn't change the psychology of confinement. I think most people that have been locked up will agree. I remember reading something on the wall of a cell I was in which said, "We are all in prison, just less confined." There is a lot of truth to that saying.

Many of the conversations in jail were centered on what happens after the release date, but most discussions were about drugs. In fact, all kinds of drugs were readily available at the center, including cocaine, marijuana, speed, and heroin. I never did any drugs while

I was doing my time. It just didn't make sense to be locked up and still committing crime; it wasn't worth the risk.

Once a week I was required to attend Narcotics Anonymous (N.A.) in the center. I didn't mind because they were usually interesting meetings. The meetings normally consisted of two people from the local N.A. chapter giving a testimony about how they were addicted to drugs, how their drug use destroyed their lives, and how joining N.A. helped them to stay clean and sober. They would refer to a higher power as the source of their strength. As I listened to the stories, I would reflect on my own past experiences. When the meetings were over, I would go back to thinking about how much crack I was going to smoke when I got released. As my release date drew nearer, I began to make plans, including buying some coke and selling rocks. I thought to myself, "This time I'm going to do it right." It's a shame that my plans didn't include doing what was necessary to get my life back on track, like getting a job and taking care of my responsibilities. The truth is, the chains of habit were still wrapped tightly around my neck, and I wasn't even trying to get free. I was still living with the pain of staying the same, but things were about to take another turn.

— Ten —

It's Time to Come Back Home

ROM THE MOMENT I was released from custody, my mind was focused on one thing and one thing only, getting a hit of crack. The incarceration served to physically separate me from the drugs, but it did nothing to diminish my desire for wanting it. I still remember taking that first hit off the pipe within hours of being released. I took in a big chest full of smoke and could immediately feel how fast my heart was pounding in my chest as I blew the smoke out. No sooner than I had blown out the smoke, I experienced a strong sense of paranoia. I became very self-conscious about what I was doing, but it was too late. One hit led to another until I was right back in the middle of the madness I had been free from for the past four months.

Since my release, I had quit my job at Burger King, was again, basically homeless, and wondering where I was going to get my next hit. I managed to get a start-up package and returned to selling rocks. Even though physically I was back in the game, my heart was no longer in it; I had lost my zeal. I constantly had an uneasy feeling, and no matter how much I drank or how much cocaine I smoked it wouldn't go away. I managed to put up a good front and kept rolling along. The truth is, I was looking at a two-and-a-half-year probation run. If at any time I was in violation, I could immediately be sent to the state penitentiary to serve out my sentence; that reality took all the fun out of getting high and taking chances.

The next day I went to Stockton where my girlfriend, Yvette, and daughter, Latoya, were living. Latoya was two years old at the time. When I arrived at the house, I didn't have much money left, and after a few days, I was flat broke again. Before heading back to Oakland to get my last paycheck from Burger King, I picked up my daughter Latoya and told her that daddy would bring her something special back. She smiled and said, "Okay Daddy!" I kissed her and left.

When I arrived back in Oakland, I made my way to the Eastmont Mall Burger King and picked up my check. I hurried over to the check-cashing place and yes you guessed it, instead of getting on the bus and heading back to Stockton, I decided to get a little cocaine to take back with me. After picking up a package, I made the mistake of taking "just one hit," and immediately, I was caught up in the madness again. The next thing I knew, I had missed the last bus to Stockton. Upon realizing this, my mind went to my daughter Latoya, and I remembered that I promised to bring her something special back. The guilt I felt was unbearable. All I could think about was that I had let her down. The more time that passed the worse I felt. I was up all-night drinking and smoking crack, but I couldn't shake the guilt.

Unconditional Love

The next morning, I caught the first bus back to Stockton. When I arrived at the large apartment complex where Latoya was staying, I remember walking down a long wide pathway leading directly to the apartment. As I got closer, I could see Latoya looking out the window. Suddenly, she was gone from the window and came out the door. I watched her as she came down the stairs, holding the rail as she hurried down. Once down the stairs, she ran as fast as her little legs would carry her, yelling, "Daddy, Daddy, Daddy!"

The chains of habit were still wrapped tightly around my neck.

I began to pick up the pace, and before I knew it, she had leaped into my open arms, hugging and squeezing me very tight. Again, I felt an overwhelming sense of guilt and shame because of how I had let Latoya down.

Latoya's response had a tremendous effect on me. I had never experienced such true unconditional love and forgiveness before. Even though it was from a little child, it still had an impact on me. That experience caused me to take a long hard look at myself. I carried the memory of that moment with me for a long time.

I was soon returned to the same old routine of drinking, smoking, and selling rocks. Even though I had to complete my probation term, I was taking chances and risking my freedom daily. The truth was, I couldn't help myself. The chains of habit were still wrapped tightly around my neck. I felt like a slave to my habit because I was miserable inside, even though I tried to keep up a good front. The guilt and pain of staying the same were catching up with me fast. I knew that I couldn't go on living "The Big Lie." The truth was, I wanted and needed to be free.

About two weeks later, I hit another financial and emotional bottom. I was basically homeless; I didn't have a place to call my own. Wherever I stayed, I could be asked to leave at any time. For the past few days, I had been hanging out with my friend Norbert, who was my source for transportation. We had been up a few days and ended up at his mother's home in the Oakland Hills. While there, I decided to call my older sister, Margaret, who lived in Redlands, California. When Margaret answered the phone, my voice revealed that all was not well with her brother; after we exchanged a few words she asked if she could pray for me. I told her, "Yes."

Margaret prayed as I had never heard anyone pray before. I may not remember her exact words, but I remember that I couldn't stop crying. She continued praying and I kept on crying. When she finally stopped praying, I promised her that if someone would purchase an airplane ticket to Ontario, California, I would take the flight. After hanging up, I fell into a deep and peaceful sleep. The prayer seemed to lift the heavy burden I had been carrying for much too long.

The Pain of Change

The next morning, I woke up emotionally torn between the harsh realities of deciding to board that plane. The decision would involve leaving the world of addiction I had become accustomed to, leaving Latoya, and bringing an end to my relationship with her mother. It also meant facing the fear of the unknown, and the dread of having to face the consequences of my poor choices over the past five years. In short, it was time to deal with the pain of change.

For the past seven years, I had lived a life of total irresponsibility and deprivation. I would now have to come face to face with the consequences of my addiction. Deep inside, I knew that I was making the right decision by leaving Oakland. My friend, Norbert, the very same person that helped me smoke up thousands of dollars in crack in the past, gave me a ride to the airport. I still considered him a true friend, because he was the same person when I had drugs and when I didn't. We were both caught up in the same nightmare, but as we made our way to the airport, we didn't exchange many words. He seemed to understand that my decision to leave Oakland was really what I needed to do. When we got to the airport, I handed him the gin bottle, we shook hands and I told him to tell everybody that I said goodbye.

As the plane taxied out for takeoff, I knew that the road ahead would not be easy. After takeoff, I looked down on the city of Oakland and thought about the destruction that was going on and would continue to go on. Although it's only a seventy-minute flight from Oakland to Ontario, it seemed like a lifetime. My mind went back over the past five-plus years. I thought about how I had intended to make a new start in Oakland, and how I had allowed my drug habit to control my life. I also thought about the many lives I helped to destroy, the going in and out of jail, the loved ones I had let down, and yes, I thought about Latoya, who I was leaving behind.

I was a shell of the man I once had been.

We drew closer to Ontario, and I thought about what was ahead in my life. The truth was, I didn't have any idea what I was going to do. I hadn't had a real job in over three years and worst of all, I was bringing my crack addiction with me to San Bernardino, California.

After landing, I began to experience an overwhelming sense of guilt and emotional uneasiness. I was going to have to face those I had hurt over the past seven years. What would I say to Sadie? How would I explain my actions to my children? What would everybody think? I had squandered homes, cars, furniture, and was literally down to the clothes on my back. I had lost my self-respect, and my self-esteem was very low, or almost non-existent. I was a shell of the man I once had been. I was a broken and wounded soul, and worse yet, I still had the chains of addiction tightly wrapped around my neck.

Since all I owned were the clothes on my back, I didn't check any luggage. I made my way to the curbside pick-up area. I remember standing there, watching others being picked up by loved ones, greeted with smiles and tears. They all seemed to be so happy. As I stood, I wondered who would be there for me? The truth was no one owed me anything.

Here I am at the curbside of Ontario International Airport where I waited for Sadie to pick me up on March 28, 1986.

Drive-By

As I stood on that curbside, I remember looking, and coming around the corner was an old Chevy Nova. Behind the wheel was Sadie, the woman I had walked out on over five years earlier. I often say, what she should have done was a drive-by, but she didn't do a drive-by. When she could have chosen to hate, she chose love, and when she could have chosen revenge, she chose to forgive. It has been said that forgiveness is like the sweet fragrance that a rose leaves on the foot that crushed it. Sadie drove up, and I got into the car, then leaned over and kissed her as if I had been on a three-day business trip. We left that airport headed down a long and difficult road to restoration.

There was no excuse for what I had done, and the guilt was tearing me up. It only got worse when I arrived at the house because my wife and children were now living in an old two-bedroom house on the rough side of town. There's no way to explain how badly I felt. I kept thinking, "This is all my fault." I wished it was a bad dream and I would soon wake up to find everything all right, but it wasn't a dream; I had to deal with the reality of the mess I made of my life, and the pain I caused in the lives of those who loved and cared about me.

House on Garner Street in San Bernardino, where Sadie and our children were living when I returned home in 1986.

My children were very glad to see me, and that made me feel a little better. It had been three years since I saw them last when Sadie brought them to visit me in Oakland. I could see that my wife had taken very good care of them in my absence. One thing that made my return less stressful was that while I was gone, Sadie did not speak negatively about me to the children. She let them know that their father was going through some things and that no matter what, I was still their father. Sadie, through that single act, revealed her true character.

I'm Still Here

That first morning in Sadie's house, I remember waking up to breakfast in bed. I couldn't even enjoy the breakfast Sadie prepared because I knew that I didn't deserve that kind of treatment. That same morning, Michelle came running into the bedroom. I asked her what was wrong, and she said, "Daddy! I just wanted to make sure that you were still here." I hugged her and assured her that I wasn't planning on going anywhere.

My children acted as though they had forgiven me for what I had done, but I could see that Sadie was struggling to come to terms with a lot of unanswered questions. I could not blame her for the way she felt because I had hurt her tremendously, and that emotional wound was still wide open. Even now, I don't know why she allowed me to return. The only thing that makes sense is that God was working out His will for our relationship, and our part was to keep walking by faith.

> *I had to deal with the reality of the mess I made of my life.*

I was glad to be back home and knew that I had to get my life back on track. I hadn't worked a steady job in over three years, except for that job at Burger King, which was only for a couple of months while I was in the Work Furlough Program. I had just been released from jail with a felony on my record. I still had the crack addiction, and worst of all, I still wanted "just one more hit!"

Although I wasn't experiencing any physical withdrawals, I did have a psychological dependence on smoking cocaine. For the first time in ten years, I had to be discreet about getting high around other people. I knew Sadie wasn't going to tolerate any form of open drug use around her house, so I went to visit a friend who knew where I could buy some rocks.

The Tweak Was On

I couldn't wait to take that first hit, so after we got everything set up, I put a hit of crack on the pipe, lit the fire, and burned it for a long time. As I inhaled the smoke, my mouth began to water. As I held the smoke in, my mind began to race, and the "tweak" was on, again.

I felt very uneasy and a heavy guilt feeling settled in. I was so paranoid that I began to imagine that the police were on their way to get me. I tried to hide my fear, but it was obvious to my friend that Dwight was "tweaking" hard. I thought maybe if I drank some gin, I would be able to shake the fear and guilt that had taken hold of my heart and mind. The truth is, I was coming under conviction, and no matter how much crack I smoked or how much gin I drank, I couldn't shake those feelings. I even tried to smile on the outside, but deep down inside I was miserable and constantly troubled in spirit. I could not find any peace in my life.

When I went back home that night, I brought a half-empty gin bottle with me. My wife knew that I had been smoking coke, and when she confronted me, I denied everything. When I tried to put the gin bottle on top of the refrigerator, Sadie grabbed it and put it in my hands and said, "You can't bring that stuff in my house." My children looked at me, and for the first time, I saw myself through their eyes, and I was ashamed. I knew I had to quit smoking, but I didn't have that inner strength or the will to do it. Like a fly caught in a spider's web, the more I struggled to get out, the more entangled in it I became.

> Worst of all, I still wanted "just one more hit.

In the weeks following, I went through the motions of trying to get my life back on track, and although I tried to put up a good front on the outside, on the inside I was a mental and emotional wreck. The guilt and shame were more than I could bear; something had to give because I couldn't bear the weight of my burdens any longer.

Eleven

Now Faith

IN HEBREWS 11:1, THE Bible says, "Now faith is the substance of things hoped for and the evidence of things not seen." This may be a nebulous concept to many, but this is the link between bondage and freedom. It is the basis for my deliverance from a life of sin, drugs, alcohol, and the morally depraved lifestyle that had become my normal. The series of events that I'm about to explain served to change the course of my life forever, because, the truth is, I have not been the same since they occurred. It's the truth that made me forever free.

I went to the unemployment office and stood around making myself available to anyone seeking a "day laborer." I managed to get a job as a landscaper in the community of Grand Terrace, California. Although it was very humbling, I had no other options and had to take whatever work I could find. One day while seeking work, an elderly man whose name was Johnny Stone, walked up to me and asked if I wanted to put some work in at his home in Grand Terrace. He decided to hire me and another young man, and we worked for $5 an hour.

When we arrived at his home, we were taken to his back yard where his dog kennels were located. He and his wife were breeders of

Australian Cattle Dogs. We cleaned around the kennels and cleared the weeds and brush from the surrounding area. After putting in a hard day's work, he drove us back to the unemployment office. As I was getting out of his truck, he asked me if I could come back the next day. Of course, I said yes, and that was the beginning of a yearlong source of employment.

Mr. Stone and I became very acquainted with one another, and he even introduced me to the owners of three other homes in the immediate area. I was soon putting in a 30 to 40-hour workweek on the hill, even though I knew I was overqualified for the type of work I was doing. The truth was, I needed to humble myself, and daily working to cultivate the earth helped me get that message.

One Friday after getting paid, I rushed home, took a shower, and quickly made it to my friend Alvin's house. I had known Alvin since I was eight years old. When I arrived, he knew what I wanted to do, so we went to pick up some crack and came back to his house. Even before we started getting high, I had an uneasy feeling on the inside, but I tried not to let it show. After I took that first hit off the pipe, the guilt set in again, I couldn't shake it. My heart was literally aching from the intensity of the guilt I was experiencing. After we got through smoking I started drinking, but the pain would not go away. Thoughts of all the misery I had caused those I loved and memories of how I had wrecked my life and the lives of so many others over the past seven years began to trouble my heart.

Pain Relief

When I left Alvin, I went straight to my sister Margaret's house. Once I got there, she was sitting in the living room watching television. She took one look at me and knew something was wrong. I paced around in her kitchen for a few minutes before telling her that I needed to talk to someone, and she knew exactly what I meant. I told her that I was feeling really bad down on the inside. She told me to come with her, and I did. I was willing to do anything if only it would relieve the pain in my heart.

We made our way to her church. When we entered the sanctuary, I noticed a few people sitting around in the choir stand. I stood waiting while she went to the pastor's office, and a few minutes later she asked me to come with her. I followed her as she led me up the stairs, past the people waiting, and back to the pastor's office. She introduced me to Pastor Herman Hubbard and left. I took a seat across from a man that I was told had, on numerous occasions, prayed for me when I didn't have the mind to pray for myself; a man that helped many members of my family through crisis after crisis, but most of all he was the man God chose to bring me to a saving knowledge of Jesus Christ.

After praying, Pastor Hubbard opened his Bible and turned to the verse in Hebrews 11:1. He read it to me, and of course, I didn't understand its total meaning. I didn't know at the time that the power was in the Word and not in my understanding. I remember

Dwight's first Pastor, Bishop Herman Hubbard, Community Baptist Church, Redlands, California. 1986

feeling so unworthy, lost, and helpless. I was so bound up in sin that I didn't feel comfortable saying the name Jesus. It seemed so unnatural to me, which gives you an idea of where I was spiritually. The years of physical and emotional stress had taken their toll on my mind and emotions.

Sick and Tired

I told Pastor Hubbard that I was tired of being addicted to drugs and I wanted to be free. I told him that I had let down everyone close to me; I had forsaken my family when they needed me the most. In short, I had lost everything, my family, my career, and my self-respect. I couldn't hold back the tears and began sobbing, as he looked on. Pastor Hubbard did his best to reassure me, and he told me that God would restore all that I had lost and would even give me more than I had before. He then said that God was going to get the glory from my life. I really couldn't relate to what he was talking about because I was hurting so bad on the inside, but I listened anyway.

The session ended with prayer, and I promised to come back in a few days. I felt much better and deep down inside I knew that everything was going to be all right. I would have to go through a few more trials before getting to the end of my sorrows.

I wish I could say that after the first meeting with Pastor Hubbard I was totally delivered and drug-free, but that would not be true. I knew that I couldn't go on living this way. I just didn't have the power to change. In fact, on my way to my second meeting with Pastor Hubbard, I made plans to get high afterward. Even as I sat in his office listening to him talk about God, I was thinking about what I was going to do after our counseling session. I had forty dollars in my pocket and was headed straight to the crack house afterward, but God had other plans.

When I left Pastor Hubbard's office, I went back to Alvin's house so that he could take me to get some rocks. Once I arrived at his house, his wife said that I had just missed him. So, I went looking for him, and for some reason, I couldn't find him anywhere. I finally just gave up and went home, with my forty dollars in my pocket. As I lay in bed that night, I knew that God was already working in my life.

I stayed drug-free until my third session with Pastor Hubbard. I hadn't used any drugs in over a week, which for me was quite an accomplishment. During our session, God was really using Pastor Hubbard because my eyes were spiritually opened. I had experienced the working of the Holy Spirit for the first time.

The Three-Way Hookup

While he was talking to me, someone came to the door and informed him that he had a long-distance phone call from Ms. Edwards. Pastor Hubbard told her to take a message, and suddenly it dawned on me that they were talking about my mother, whose last name was Edwards. When I mentioned it to Pastor Hubbard, he immediately picked up the phone. Once he realized it was my mother, he turned on the speakerphone, so that I could hear my mother's voice. When I recognized it, a lump formed in my throat, and tears came to my eyes. My mother was thanking and commending Pastor Hubbard for working with me. He then interrupted her and motioned for me to say something. I said, "Hi Mama," she immediately recognized my voice and let us know that she was surprised to hear it. They say that coincidence is God's way of remaining anonymous. This three-way hookup served as a sign that God's hand was truly at work in my life. I think Pastor Hubbard was moved by what happened as well.

Although I had an intellectual understanding of what it meant to be saved by God, I didn't have the spiritual strength to overcome the strong desire for smoking cocaine. I also knew that I really wanted to be drug-free, but I wasn't able to totally surrender to God's power to set me free until the 3rd Friday in June 1986. As I had done on many occasions, I got paid and went to my friend's house to get high. When I ran out of drugs and money, I still wanted just one more hit. The truth is most crack addicts seem to have an insatiable bottomless pit of desire for more and more. The big problem is most of the time their craving outlasts their money to buy more, and when that happens, they get very creative when it comes to how they are going to come up with more money.

> " *I didn't have the spiritual strength to overcome the strong desire for smoking cocaine.* "

Alvin and I decided to visit my youngest sister, Angela, who lived in Rialto, California at the time. I had barely got in her front door before I literally began begging her to give me twenty dollars. She didn't want to give me the money because she knew what I was going to do with it. After getting the money, Alvin and I went directly to the crack house and purchased one last package, and headed back to Redlands.

We finally ended up at a house across the street from my sister, Margaret, who was away in New Jersey attending her son, Clifford's, high school graduation. I was glad she wasn't home because it would have added to my paranoia. We quickly made our way into her neighbor's house and found a room we could smoke in. A few other people were getting high as well. Since we didn't have much, we took our time and divided the dove rock up and started smoking. In less than twenty minutes we finished our ritual, and before too long as you might imagine, we wanted more.

One of my nephews happened to be in the next room, and he had rocks for sale. I went to him and asked for some drugs on credit. He immediately said, "No Uncle Dwight, you have had enough." Refusing to take no for an answer, I remember going back over to him saying, "Please, just give me one hit." While begging for that hit, I was becoming very self-conscious about how I was acting so desperate for that hit of crack. He reluctantly gave me the small hit and left the room. I took the hit and walked over to a barstool, sat down and put the hit on the pipe, stuck the fire to it, and took in a big chest full of smoke. I then leaned back, looked up, blew the smoke out, and watched it stream all the way up to the ceiling. I put the pipe down, stood up, and headed for the front door.

That's It!

After walking out the door, I turned to my friend, Alvin, and said, "That's it, I'm done." I think he thought I meant that I was through for the night and we would hook up the next day. What he didn't know was that something was going on in my heart. As I began walking across the street to my sister's house, I felt an unbearable sense of guilt and shame set in. It seemed as though all the wrong I had done began to flood my mind, and I couldn't bear the weight of it all.

I walked into my sister's house and got as far as her hallway, just inside the door, and I slumped down and curled up on the floor. I began to cry out to God, asking him to set me free from the bondage of that addiction. I had truly come to the end of my road and was surrendering my will to God's power. I don't know how long I was rolling around on that floor, but what I do know is that when I got up off the floor, I had a sense that the chains of addiction had been broken. The Truth had finally made me free! Praise the Lord! That third Friday in June 1986 was the very last time I smoked crack.

When I had left home that morning, foremost on my mind was how I was going to get high after work. That's exactly what I did. What I didn't anticipate was that it was all a set up for a defining moment of change. That moment came when I was put in a position to see and own who I had become. At that same moment, the truth lifted me up, and I have not been the same since. When I returned home that night and crawled into the bed with my wife. She had no idea that the drug-addicted husband who left home that morning was returning home clean, sober, and drug-free.

The days that followed were filled with a new sense of purpose and determination. I began to notice that when I woke up each morning my thoughts were not on how I was going to get high. I began to think about doing good and changing my life. I began to have a hunger for learning more about the teachings in the Bible.

If you asked me to explain how it happened, I couldn't begin to tell you. I only know something had truly changed on the inside of me. I had the inner peace my mother had always talked about. I was able to accept the fact that I had made many wrong decisions in my life, disappointed many people, and had made a real mess of things, but most of all I understood that because of what Jesus did on the cross, in God's sight I was forgiven. The burden of my sins was lifted, and I felt good deep down in my soul. Yes, I was happy, happy, happy!

Twelve

Under Christian Experience

I REMEMBER THE DAY I decided to join Community Baptist Church of Redlands California. When I got up that Sunday morning I planned to come forward when the invitation was given to become a member of the church. After giving his sermon that morning Pastor Hubbard immediately went back to his office. As he was leaving the platform, he instructed one of his associate ministers, Rev. Darrell Hudson, to give the invitation and to open the doors of the church.

As soon as I heard the words, "The doors of the church are open," I got up, walked forward, and took a seat. As I sat there facing the congregation, the clerk came over and asked me if I was coming for prayer, baptism, or under Christian experience. I replied, "Under Christian Experience." It is those three words that are the sum total of my new life and walk of faith. My drug rehab program would be carried out within the confines of my church attendance and participation in the activities available for helping me to grow mentally, physically, and most of all, spiritually.

I could have gone to a secular drug rehabilitation program for help. If I had sat down for an intake session and told a drug and alcohol counselor that for the past seven years I had smoked cocaine every chance I got and drank alcohol nearly every day, they would have probably recommended me to a minimum of six months in-house treatment for chemical dependency. And, there was no guarantee that I would be cured.

Once I made a decision to follow the teachings of Jesus Christ, and gave Him control of my life, in only a matter of days, I noticed that my desire for many of the self-destructive habits I had begun to dissipate more and more as time went by.

The more I exposed myself to the positive messages of hope and inner healing, the more I experienced tangible transformation. My entire focus on what I thought was important had changed. Words cannot explain the feeling I had on the inside. I can only characterize it by saying it was as though I had been "born again". I no longer counted my past life as being anything of value; it was a bitter legacy of the "Old Dwight."

Having made a decision to give God a chance in my life, I accepted the fact that it wasn't going to be easy, but it was going to be necessary. I would be walking into a completely unfamiliar arena. I had been a lot of things in my life, but I had never been a practicing Christian. I have followed many people and many ideas, but I had never followed Jesus. I wondered if my life would suddenly get boring and I would stop enjoying life. My idea of a Christian was someone that didn't drink, smoke, or curse, and most of all didn't have any fun. I knew that I had to give it a try because I couldn't continue going down the destructive path of addiction.

I was about to begin my walk of faith, believing that everything was going to be all right. One thing I did know was that I couldn't go back to my old way of thinking and living. With that in mind, let me share with you the early days of my walk of faith.

A Drug-Free Summer

The summer of 1986 was special for many reasons. First, it was a drug-free summer, and I was working at a real job for a living and that was a big change for me. Even though I was seriously seeking a better job, for some reason I was unable to find one in my trained profession, which was Real Estate Sales and clerk duties. So, as I shared earlier, I had to settle for a job as a landscaper. Yes, I would be doing yard work. I was pulling weeds, chopping down tall bushes, trimming hedges, painting, cleaning, and whatever else needed to be done. It wasn't what I wanted to do, but it was what God used to get the message across, that I needed to get back down to earth, literally.

As I worked in the hot summer sun, I was able to think about many things. Since I was alone, and there was nobody but me and the Lord. I would think about the stories I read in the Bible and the teachings I had heard while attending Bible class. I thought back on what my life was like before making a decision to change. I often thought about the many destructive deeds I did while chasing the crack pipe and living a selfish life of sin and disobedience. I frequently thanked God for giving me a second chance and the opportunity to live a life free from drugs and other destructive habits. I shed many tears of regret and tears of gratitude while I was pulling those weeds and performing odd jobs for $5.00 an hour.

After three months, Pastor Hubbard asked me to conduct a series of anti-drug rallies once a month. While working on the hill, I spent time thinking about what I was going to speak about, leading up to each rally. I had such a sense of freedom while I was working on the hill in Grand Terrace. I was able to sweat out the impurities accumulated in my body during my years of drug and alcohol abuse.

I kid you not; I could literally see the impurities coming through the pores on my arms and upper body.

Working on that hill was also a very humbling experience. I had to put aside my pride and perform what I considered menial tasks. It turned out that this type of work was the best therapy I could have had. Because as I chopped away at those weeds, I was able to think about where I had gone wrong over the past seven years.

Out of the Sun

I spent about a year working as a landscaper on that hill before I was able to get another job working at the Riverside Book Bindery, a business owned by three Christians. They were nice people that believed in working long, hard hours. They expected their employees to do the same.

I was so glad to come in out of the hot "Grand Terrace" sun, I didn't mind putting in the long hours. I must say that I had never had to engage in so much tedious work in my entire life. I had to gather, sort, stack, and bind seemingly endless reams of paper, but I hung in there. I saw it as a test that God was taking me through before giving me something better. God likes to make sure that we can be faithful over little things before he trusts us with bigger and better things. It's sort of like God's merit system (Matthew 25:23).

An elderly lady named Margaret, the mother of one of the owners was frequently at the bindery. She was a very kind and spiritual woman with a beautiful head of gray hair, and the most piercing blue eyes I had ever seen. Margaret encouraged me to memorize verses in the Bible. She always had a kind word to say. I sensed that she really did love the Lord. This job lasted about three months before I went to my next assignment. Even though the hours were long, and I left there very tired, I continued to study the Bible, attended Bible class on Wednesday, and worship services on Sunday. What I'm trying to say is that when I made up my mind that I wanted to be free, it didn't matter what kind of job I had because through it all I knew that God was continuing to work out His will for my life, and I was enjoying the journey.

I found myself looking forward to Sunday services; I tried not to miss even one. When I would be in the church service, my mind would go back to when I was in Oakland running the streets day and night smoking and selling drugs. I would think about the dangerous situations I got myself into and I thought about the times I spent in jail. I thought about the sense of hopelessness I once felt and how it was only by the grace of God that I made it out of that nightmare alive. Many times, I would just sit there and shed tears of thanksgiving and pure joy.

Mother Johnston's Miracle

Let me share an experience that occurred early in my Christian walk. This experience had a tremendous effect on the building up of my faith in God. Up until this time I heard people say that God is a miracle worker. I believed that God could work miracles because I had read about the many miracles He had performed in biblical times. I had never actually witnessed a miracle with my own eyes, but the next three days would change that.

It was the summer of 1987 and I had to see Pastor Hubbard about a personal matter. When I got off work, I went to the church. As I walked up to the door at the pastor's office, I wasn't sure if he was in, so I just knocked and to my surprise, he said, "Come in." After entering, I could see that something was on his mind because he greeted me with a forced smile. He then asked me if I would go someplace with him. I said, "Yes." After grabbing his hat and Bible, we were on our way. As he drove along not much was said, so I sensed that we were on a serious mission.

When we arrived at our destination, Pastor Hubbard motioned for me to come with him. After finding the apartment we were looking for, I was still in the dark about what was going on. A young lady greeted us at the door and led us straight into a bedroom where her grandmother, Mother Johnston was lying down. As I turned the corner and entered the room, I laid eyes upon the elderly woman lying in bed, with a very distressed look on her face. I noticed that she was connected up to an oxygen machine with a tube in her nose. I learned that she was suffering from terminal cancer and the doctors had done all they could and sent her home to die. They gave her no more than three days to live. So, there she lay, body racking in pain from cancer eating away on her body, even the morphine was not enough to totally quench her pain.

As we stood at Mother Johnston's bedside Pastor Hubbard began to speak with her. I heard him say that God would get the glory out of the situation. When I heard him say that, I thought to myself, "How can God get any glory out of a woman dying of cancer?" I just stood quietly and watched as Pastor Hubbard continued to minister to Mother Johnston. Suddenly Pastor Hubbard leaned over and looked into Mother Johnston's eyes and said, "Mother I don't like the way your eyes are looking". I leaned over and noticed that she seemed to have a thick dull gray film over her eyes. Pastor immediately began praying, he prayed with power, commanding Satan to be gone, in the name of Jesus. As I prayed with him, it seemed as if I was going to explode from the presence of the power of God in the room. When he finally said "Amen", I opened my eyes and looked at Mother Johnston. As she opened her eyes, I noticed a crystal-clear sparkle in them. Whatever she had over her eyes before the prayer was clearly gone, and I saw this transformation with my own eyes.

Truly God had moved in a mighty way. Before praying it seemed as if death was trying to overtake her. It was as if God was saying, "Not now, not now." Mother Johnston said that she felt much better. I had never seen anything like that in my life. Praise the Lord.

Before we left, Pastor Hubbard said that he wanted her to come to the Revival taking place at the church the following week and that he wanted to pick her up for church the next day. She smiled and said that if she started to feel better, she would try. We promised to return the next day and left the house. I remember thinking to myself, "This woman is supposed to be dead in three days, and here we are, planning to pick her up for church tomorrow."

The next day when we arrived at Mother Johnston's home, we found out that her condition had gotten worse. She couldn't hold down anything she ate or drank, so was not able to take her pain medication. She was very close to death that day. We under-

I was able to sweat out the impurities accumulated in my body.

stood when she said that she wouldn't be able to make it to church that night. So, after having a word of prayer, we left promising to return the next day. We went on to church and after the message was preached, Pastor Hubbard called on all who would pray and fast for Mother Johnston. We were told to go without food or water, which was something that I had never done voluntarily, but I was willing to do it for Mother Johnston.

Getting through the next day was tough, but I did it. That evening I was to meet Pastor Hubbard at Mother Johnston's house. I arrived a little early and just had a seat in the front room. When Pastor Hubbard arrived, he brought with him, Reverend Roy Harris, and two nurses from the church. The nurses went back to the bedroom, as we sat waiting patiently for our date to get ready. Finally, the door opened, and we were asked to come into the bedroom. As we walked in, Mother Johnston was sitting in her wheelchair. When she turned around, we beheld a beautiful lady, face glowing and she was smiling from ear to ear. I couldn't believe my eyes, the woman doctors said would be dead in three days was instead on her way to church, and very much alive.

When we arrived at the church, the service was already in progress. When the doors were swung open and I wheeled Mother Johnston in, all heads turned to see her. The preacher even stopped in the middle of his message, to recognize her. It was a moment I shall never forget because God had truly worked a miracle that night. When I looked around and saw many with tears in their eyes, my mind went back to that first night I saw Mother Johnston, when Pastor Hubbard said, "God must get the glory." I now understood what he meant, and my faith in God was strengthened.

The experience I have just shared with you is one of many that I have witnessed since becoming a Christian. My life was once meaningless and empty and going down a dead-end street. Since I began my walk of faith, each day is a new experience of growing in the knowledge of the grace of God, and it's all "Under Christian Experience."

---- Thirteen ----

A Praying Mother

IT WAS IN THE summer of 1988, I was into my third year on the Christian battlefield. For some time God had been speaking to my heart about what He wanted me to do in His service. God was communicating to me in such a way that I knew He was calling me into the ministry of the gospel. I had been working in the church as what's called a "Deacon on a trial" and I was scheduled to be officially ordained on July 24, 1988.

The Saturday before I was to be ordained as a Deacon, the Teen Department was having a car wash fundraiser, and I stopped by to give them a donation. As I was waiting for my car to be washed, I saw Pastor Hubbard standing under a shade tree talking to some church members. I walked over to say hello to him and we had a brief conversation. As I was about to leave, Pastor Hubbard asked me to meet him at the church in about an hour, and I told him that I would be there.

Even though I hadn't said anything to him about me being called into the ministry, I had a feeling that Pastor Hubbard was going to question me about it. When the Pastor got to the church we went to his office. After having a word of prayer he asked me if I felt that God was calling me into the ministry? Without hesitation, I said, "Yes."

We then had a word of prayer in which God confirmed the calling to the Pastor. I remember feeling somewhat emotional while listening to Pastor Hubbard as he gave me an understanding of what it meant to be called into the ministry. As he was speaking to me, I couldn't hold back the tears. I raised my Bible to my face and just cried tears of thanksgiving to God. I left the church that day one of the happiest men on earth. I just couldn't stop praising God.

No Ordinary Ordination

Sunday, July 24, 1988, had finally come for the Deacon Ordination Ceremony and I was excited about it. Family members and friends from all over were going to be there. The Deacons were dressed in black suits and white shoes. As I sat waiting for the ceremony to begin, I kept looking over my shoulder at many of my family members in attendance. They were all sitting in one section of the church. They all knew my story and were glad that I was trying to change my life.

Even my former business partner, and Heisman Trophy winner, Johnny Rodgers was there with his son Terry. Everybody seemed happy for me. Finally, the time came for the ordination ceremony to begin. The candidates were led out of the church into the vestibule and were called in one at a time to be examined. My name was called first and I was escorted in by two other Deacons. As we walked down the long aisle, I was just thanking God for saving my soul and establishing me in the church.

When we made it to the front of the church, I was placed in a chair before the altar and asked a series of questions. I was able to answer all of them correctly. Pastor Hubbard then came down and laid hands on me and prayed. I was then taken and given a seat with the other Deacons. God had made a deacon out of a drug addict. Praise the Lord!

The next thing that happened came as a complete surprise to everyone because we were sitting there waiting for Pastor Hubbard to start his sermon, but he began talking about a person who was being called into the ministry. He wouldn't say whom he was referring to. As I kept listening, I thought he was talking about one of the other deacons, until he said something that let me know he was talking about me. Instantly, I felt my heart begin to beat faster with each moment.

Unspeakable Joy

Pastor Hubbard said he was going to come down to get the person and bring them up to the rostrum. As he came down, he went to the other end of the pew where the deacons were sitting. He got directly in front of Deacon Collins, then made a sharp turn and came straight to me, grabbed my hand and pulled me up, and started towards the rostrum, but after taking two steps the Holy Spirit came upon me and I started leaping and shouting for joy. I could not contain the joy that had been stirred up in me. It's hard to explain what I was experiencing, but I do know that I felt free way down deep in my soul.

When I finally stopped praising God, I was overtaken by family members and friends as they expressed their love and support for me. Many had tears in their eyes, even Johnny Rodgers was overwhelmed by his emotions. Once things calmed down, I walked up and sat down with the rest of the Ministers. God had truly brought me a mighty long way, and I was very grateful. Over the next few weeks, I received some basic guidelines and instructions on how to prepare a sermon. At my third session with Pastor Hubbard, I was given a date on which I was to preach my first sermon, Sunday, October 2, 1988, at Community Baptist Church, in Redlands, California.

It was 7:30 P.M. and I had been preparing for this night for nearly two months. I was seated with the other ministers and looking out into the audience, and of course, I saw many familiar faces. I saw my grandmother, Mirdis Roby, my mother, Luvenia, four of my sisters, three aunts, some cousins, nieces, nephews, and friends. I was especially glad that Dwight II and Michelle were there. I wished that my wife had been in attendance, but I understood that some things just needed more time.

The deacons had just ended a very spiritual devotion and Pastor Hubbard began his pastoral remarks. He was giving the audience a brief history of how I became a believer. As I sat listening, my heart was filled with thanksgiving, because I never dreamed that I would one day be sitting and waiting to preach for the very first time. I knew that I didn't deserve such an honor, but I was eternally glad that it was about to become a reality.

Following the pastoral remarks, Dr. Hubbard motioned for me to come back to his office. When we got into his office, he told me to have a seat in his chair behind the desk, and after praying, gave me an understanding that I was to allow God to have his way when I preach and not to worry about what he or anyone else thought. His words really set me at ease, and I felt relaxed. He then told me to come out when I thought I was ready. After he left I prayed and asked God to humble me and let His word go forth with power and

> I never dreamed that I would one day be waiting to preach.

clarity. I could hear the choir singing praises to God, so I got up, took a deep breath, came back out, and returned to my seat.

I was nervous but I knew that God was in control and everything would be just fine. When the choir was done singing, Pastor Hubbard got up and called up a friend of mine from the Oakland Bay Area. He was Elder Greg D. Williams, a person I met in Oakland while still in my addiction. We had smoked cocaine together and made a wreck of our lives in much the same way. It was good to see how God had changed my friend, and how He was using Greg as a living testimony of His saving power. Greg shared a few words about how we had met and how we were reunited after both our lives took a turn for the better. Then I heard him say, "It gives me great pleasure to introduce to some and present to others, my friend, Rev. Dwight Pledger." I stood up and we embraced in brotherly love and as a verification of our deep friendship as brothers in Christ.

A Praying Mother

It was a very surreal moment looking out on the congregation. I shared some opening remarks, thanking everyone for being there to support me. After opening in prayer, I read my scripture text, and gave my sermon title, "A Praying Mother." I felt a little emotional just saying those words because while I was living that dangerous lifestyle, my mother fasted and prayed for me without ceasing. I wanted her to know that I was grateful for the unconditional love she extended to me, even when I didn't deserve it.

While I was delivering the message, the congregation was very engaged and verbally responsive, because I heard quite a few "Amens" as I shared the Word. I stayed close to my notes and managed to cover most of what I had studied. As I drew the message to a close,

I shared a story about a praying mother and an "old no-good son." I began by saying:

> There was a praying mother who gave birth to a bouncing baby boy; she raised him all by herself. As time passed this boy grew up and even graduated from high school. It looked like this boy was going to be all right, until something happened, and he began to change. He got hooked up with the wrong crowd and began to get into trouble with the law. Because this praying mother loved that boy, she told him that since he wasn't going to change, he had to go. So that old no-good son went and joined the Navy, and it again looked like he was going to be all right. He got married and began to move up in life. One day that praying mother came to that old no-good son and said, "Son you know the Lord is really blessing you, and you ought to give your heart to Jesus; you ought to give God some of your time, and some of your money." That old no-good son looked at his mama real crazy and said, "I don't want to hear about your Jesus. I don't have any time and I'm sure not giving my hard-earned money to no preacher." So that praying mother went on back home.
>
> That old no-good son kept on moving up in life. He bought some fine cars, moved into a big beautiful house, and hung out with the "in crowd." One day that praying mother came back to visit that old no-good son and she repeated the same words she told him before, she said, "Son you know the Lord is really blessing you, and you ought to give your

heart to Jesus; you ought to give God some of your time and some of your money." That old no-good son looked at his mother real crazy and said in so many words, "I don't want to hear about your Jesus. I don't have time and am not giving up any of my hard-earned money." So that praying mother went on back home.

Not long after that, things took a turn for the worse cause that old no-good son got hooked on drugs. It wasn't long before that old no-good son lost his fine cars, big house, and even walked out on his wife and children, all in the name of cocaine. When that praying mother heard the news, it hurt her very much, but she kept on praying for that old no-good son. Every time she went to church, she would go to the altar, carrying the burden of the old no-good son on her back. When she got to the altar, she would lay her son on the altar and cry out to the Lord, asking Him to deliver her son and save his soul. When she got through praying, she would lean over and pick up her son, put him on her back, and carry him on back home with her.

That old no-good son only got worse. He was selling and using drugs, going in and out of jail, but that mother kept on praying. She went back to the altar still carrying the burden of that old no-good son on her back. When she got there this time, she laid her son on the altar, then got down on her knees and cried out to the Lord, asking Him to deliver her son and save his soul. When she got up off her knees, she leaned over and picked up her son, and carried him back home with her.

Things only got worse for that old no-good son. So that praying mother decided to go for a visit. She wanted to see her boy for herself so she got on an airplane. When she got there somebody came upstairs and told that old no-good son that his mother was downstairs. He was shocked and ashamed of himself, but he went to her anyway. When he got to where she was, his mother stood up, took one look at her son and she knew that there was nothing she could do for him. After saying a few words to that old no-good son, he told his mother that he had to leave, but he would be right back.

He never did make it back, so that praying mother went back home. She had seen with her own eyes that her son was in trouble, but she kept on praying for that old no-good son. She went back to the altar carrying that old no-good son on her back. When she got to the altar, she laid that old no-good son down on the altar. She got down on her knees and began to pray, "Lord, I've done all that I can, and I can't do anymore, so I give him to you Lord, he is in Your hands." When she got through praying, she stood up, with tears in her eyes, and instead of picking that old no-good son up, she turned and walked away. After taking a few steps, she turned and took one last look at that old no-good son on the altar, and then she went on back home.

I concluded the story by saying, "I'll tell you why I know so much about that old no-good son because I am that old no-good son. I walked over to my mother and said, "And here's my praying mother." Even as I was pointing to her the Spirit of the Lord fell upon the church bringing joy, joy, joy. I went over and took my mother into my arms, and we just hugged until it seemed as though we had become one in the Spirit.

This is my favorite photo with my mother, Luvenia, taken in Kansas City, Missouri at the Wiley/Shine family reunion in July 1986.

When things finally calmed down, Pastor Hubbard began to introduce my family. Starting with my grandmother, Mirdis Roby, who went on to live to the age of one hundred and five. He then introduced my mother, Luvenia Edwards, and handed her the microphone. This is what she had to say:

As always, I'm so happy to be in the house of God. I am doubly happy tonight to see what a mother's prayers will do. As Dwight said, when you carry it, God can't do what needs to be done, but when you turn it over to the Lord... When Dwight called me and I could tell him that I was at peace, tonight is living proof that he wanted that peace. He needs Jesus more now than ever because the devil is so angry and is going to throw every stumbling block in his way. He's going to block him on every side, but Jesus lives.

When Dwight was out there in the world, there were two songs that would come to mind. The first is, 'Because He Lives (I Can Face Tomorrow)' and to all of you that are here tonight, because He lives you can face tomorrow. The next song is, 'It Is No Secret (What God Can Do)'. Many times, in the midnight hour, when I couldn't sleep, I would hum that little song. Hold onto that everybody. I don't care how low you fall or how low your children fall, God knows about it! God cares about it! He said there is nothing in this world that can separate us from Him. We separate ourselves from Him, but God is always there, and His hands are forever outstretched. And to the young people here tonight, drugs are not where it's at, but Jesus is where it's at. When you hold onto Jesus, and I know what I'm talking about, when you hold onto Him, in the midnight hour and you can't sleep when everybody else is asleep, call on Him whether you are young, or old. His ears are forever listening, thank you."

My mother after her first ride in a limousine at the celebration of her 75th birthday, a truly precious memory that I will always treasure.

Since the writing of this book, my mother made her transition from earth to Glory on December 7, 2016, and is now enjoying a sabbath that will have no end. Thank you, Mama, for praying for me!

—— *Fourteen* ——

Restoration

A T THIS WRITING, IT has been over thirty years since I stepped off the airplane at Ontario International Airport. I had just the clothes I was wearing on my back and the chains of habit still wrapped tightly around my neck in the form of a seven-year crack cocaine addiction, five-years of it separated from my wife and children. In addition to that, I had to leave my two-year-old daughter, Latoya, in Northern California. What I want you to see in this chapter is that once I turned my life over to Jesus Christ, God began the process of restoring my family, relationships, health, career, finances, and more. I give God the praise for what His grace has done for me. I also want to thank God for the countless number of people He has used to encourage, bless, and restore my life.

If you are reading this book and your life is in need of restoration, just know that God is no respecter of persons. What He did in my life, He is able to do in yours. I just want to be an example of what's possible for all who dare to have a strong desire for change and restoration in their life.

Family Restored

I was away from my wife and children for over five years and I managed to burn many bridges due to my addiction and selfish nature. While in Oakland, I did a lot of damage to many relationships there as well; some will never be repaired, and others I have asked God to forgive me for whatever wrong I committed while running the streets in the Bay Area and living a life of sin.

Even though Sadie allowed me to come to her house and treated me better than I deserved, it took a very long time for us to readjust to each other. It wasn't until I became totally free from drugs and alcohol that I was even able to focus on rebuilding my relationship with her and our children.

Another primary concern that weighed heavy on my heart was my daughter, Latoya, who was still living in Northern California with her mother, Yvette. Sadie's attitude about Latoya, who was two years old at the time, was that Latoya shouldn't be punished for something that was out of her control. Sadie consented to Latoya coming to spend the summers and other holidays with us in Southern California. Yvette allowed her to visit on many occasions. When Latoya turned 13, she came to live with us permanently. I am grateful to Sadie and Yvette for how they handled the care of Latoya because they both prioritized her needs above their pride or pain.

The first family portrait that included my daughter Latoya, the summer of 1986, taken in San Bernardino, California.

To say I carried a lot of guilt would be an understatement. Even though I knew that God, Sadie, and I believed my children, had forgiven me, I still carried tons of regret for abandoning them while in my addiction. I was also determined to make things work by doing what I had in my power to do. Over time we continued to grow closer as a family unit, dealing with issues as they came up, and never losing our trust in God to do what only He had the power to do. What I learned was that forgiveness can be granted in a moment but rebuilding trust takes time, and it refuses to be rushed.

Proud Pops

The good news is Sadie and I have been back together for over 34 years, and by the grace of God, we recently celebrated our 48th wedding anniversary. Dwight, and his wife, Melody, have raised six of our grandchildren: Alyssa, Jaslene, Theresa, Marayah, Joseph, and Dwight, III. Dwight and Melody have a growing trucking business. Michelle is the Diversity, Equity, and Integration Director and faculty member at High Tech High's Graduate School of Education. She travels nationally and internationally, delivering keynotes and facilitating professional development. In 2018 she earned her Doctorate in Education. Latoya and her husband Usbaldo and parents to our youngest grandson, Christopher. Latoya has also earned two master's degrees, a teaching credential, and is now a Special Education teacher. Our granddaughter Alyssa gave birth to twin boys, Roland and Ryder, making Sadie and me, great-grandparents. All of our children, grandchildren, and great-grandchildren have made Sadie and me "Godly-proud" in so many ways. We as a family have so much to be thankful for, and we should never forget what God has done for all of us.

When I was caught up in my addiction and living a totally irresponsible life, I lost the close relationship I once had with my five sisters and one brother. Over time, even those relationships have been restored. I thank them all for their prayers, both while I was in my addiction, and during the restoration period with my family. When I was living a dangerous life as a drug dealer, my family was praying that I would one day be set free. They continued to pray until prayer changed things.

Dwight's mother, grandmother, and siblings at the 100th birthday celebration of Mirdis Roby seated left. Luvenia Edwards seated right and standing left to right, Loretta Smith, Margaret Winn, Angela Jones, Dwight Pledger, Alice Roberts, Brenda James, Jerome Miller. Pine Bluff, Arkansas 2003.

Even though my mother never gave up on me, I often think back on the day she released me into the hands of the Lord. It was a few weeks before I went to jail. I had been up all night and was feeling depressed. I called my mother who was living in Arkansas. Many times, when I called her, I would talk about all the problems I was having in my life; she would get emotional, which would cause me to get emotional, and we would have a big pity party.

Goodbye…

On this occasion, she had a different tone in her voice, she sounded like she was very happy. I began to get emotional and explain how bad I was feeling about my life. My mother interrupted me and said, "Son I have prayed everything I could think to pray for you and there is nothing else I can do." She added, "I'm happy, and if I don't ever see you again, I'm at peace." She then said, "Goodbye my son," and hung up the phone. That conversation shook me up. I thought long and hard about how I was living my life. It wasn't long after that phone call that I took that plane ride back to Southern California and changed my life. This incident was the inspiration for the story I shared about the "Praying Mother and the Old No-Good Son."

Oftentimes, when I speak with mothers and fathers who are dealing with children or loved ones living an out of control lifestyle, I share that story. I let them know that when my mother informed me that she would no longer allow my poor life choices to stress her out, she helped me to come to terms with the changes I needed to make in my own life. After I was converted and drug-free, my mother and I had many long conversations about God and the many things that were going on in my life. We were able to relate to each other as equal adults, with our own lives and opinions about life.

Mama and I enjoyed each other for another 30 years before she went home to be with the Lord; may she rest in Heaven. I'm so glad that she had a chance to see me get clean, sober, and restored to my family. I really disappointed her when I took a wrong turn in life.

She had done her best to raise us to be honest and well-behaved children. She had always put her children first and prayed for us until her dying day. I miss Mama more than you can imagine, and I think of her every day, in one way or another. The strength of her prayers is still with us until this day.

Mr. Pledge

My father's name is Allen King Pledger. He married my mother in 1952, which was the year of my birth. By the time I was two years old, he and my mother divorced, and I would not see him again until I was twenty-three years old. I grew up with no childhood memories of him, not even so much as a photograph. Mama did not like talking about him, except to say that when he started to physically abuse her, she left him and went her separate way. So, for the next twenty-one years, I accepted the fact that I would grow up without his presence in my life. His absence did not stop me from thinking about and wondering what it would be like to meet and know him. One of the stories I told myself is that I was better off without him because most of my friends who grew up with a father in the home were not any happier than I was at the time.

When I was about ten years old, I remember getting a bicycle delivered to our home in the projects of Redlands. I was told that my father had bought it for me. I was so happy to get that shiny new red bicycle; and I went all over the projects telling everyone that my father bought me a bicycle. Many years later I found out the truth. It was actually my grandmother Mirdis who bought me that bike because she felt sorry that I had never heard from my father. So evidently, I must have said something to her about how I felt about my father not being in my life.

People often say, "There is a first time for everything," and I was about to experience one of the most important first times of my entire life. In January 1976, while still serving in the Navy, I traveled to Patrick Air Force Base, in Cocoa Beach, Florida to attend the Department of Defense Race Relations Institute (DRRI), to train as an Equal Opportunity Program Specialist. I would later become a part of the Navy's effort to implement its Navy-wide race relations programs. While attending school at DRRI, I received word that my father was living in a city called Goulds, located in southern Florida. Keep in mind that I had never even

Forgiveness can be granted in a moment but rebuilding trust takes time.

seen a photo of my father, and now I was only a few hours from his home. Just the thought that I might meet my father for the first time caused my mind to race in many directions. "What would he look like? What would I say to him? Would he even want to see me?"

Although I did not have his address, I was able to contact someone who knew where my father was living. About two weeks later Tommy, a fellow classmate, drove me down to Coral Gables where I met the man who could take me to see my father. Tommy and I drove this man to where he said my father was living. I remember pulling up to a spot, and after getting out of the car, we had to walk a short distance to my father's house. As we were walking, I was trying to wrap my mind around what was about to happen. I was twenty-three years old, and I was about to meet my seventy-eight-year-old father for the very first time.

We walked up to the door, knocked, and when my father opened the door the man who brought us there said, "Mr. Pledge, this is your son, Dwight." My father looked straight into my eyes, I fixed my eyes on his eyes, and at that moment, we instantly connected as father and son. It was as if twenty-one years of distance diminished, and it became a defining moment that would forever change my perspective on life going forward. In an instant, I took note of his eyes, his nose, his slim build, and his

> " I chose to enjoy every moment I had, just being in my father's presence. "

warm friendly smile. We embraced, and our relationship was off to a memorable start. I was so glad to see him, and do not remember having one bit of anger or bitterness toward him. I was just so elated that I had finally met and spoken with my father, my dad, Allen King Pledger, who they called "Mr. Pledge."

Over the next two months, I managed to visit and spend time with my father. We talked about many things during those visits. Questions like "Why did you leave me?" or "Why didn't you come back to visit me?" never came up in our conversation. They didn't come up, because, at that time, it really didn't matter. His answer would not have changed one thing about our past. I chose to enjoy every moment I had, just being in my father's presence. We talked about where he was born, what his father's name was, and his family roots. I also brought him up to speed on my family and told him about the training I was receiving at the Race Relations Institute.

At that time, I did not have an interest in spiritual things, but he would talk to me about God, and the need to change my life and get on the right path. His spiritual journey had taken him from being a Catholic, a Jehovah's Witnesses, and finally a Christian, and he worshipped at a church named Morning Star Baptist Church.

He must have been some kind of Elder or Minister in the church because I remember him preparing a message for the upcoming Easter Sunday service.

On one of my visits, he even shared one of his messages with me, and I recorded it. I remember him quoting long verses out of the book of Genesis, and I later found out that he had memorized entire chapters of the Bible. I captured quite a few quotations on my cassette recorder but lost them in the process of my many moves from house to house. To this day, I wish there was a way to recover those lost cassettes. I came to visit a couple more times before my school ended, and I had to return to California. I don't quite remember what I said to my dad when I left, but I think I promised to return soon to see him again, and we talked about the possibility of him coming to visit me in California.

Once back in California, I was especially glad to see Dwight II who was then ten-months-old. He had contracted a septic hip problem, was operated on, and then given a special hip brace to wear that went from his waist down. Sadie and I had been married for almost four years, and we were enjoying our son and the San Diego lifestyle. I was up for a promotion to E-6, which would include a nice pay raise. I had also begun selling real estate part-time and was beginning to scale up my income considerably.

It became a defining moment that would forever change my perspective.

About three weeks had gone by since my return from the training in Florida. I remember receiving a phone call from Ms. Isabel, who was a friend of my father. Ms. Isabel was calling to tell me that my father had died suddenly. I thanked her for calling, hung up the phone, and shared the news with my wife. Then, I calmly walked into our bedroom, laid across the bed, and the tears began to flow. It was a deep hurtful cry. I remember thinking how unfair it was to lose my father so soon after getting to know him for the first time. It was a heavy loss and it took a while to release twenty-three years of loss and disappointment. The next day I made arrangements to travel back to Florida for my father's funeral services.

Blood

Once back in Florida I connected with some family on my father's side. My oldest brother James Pledger flew in from Los Angeles, California. I also met my sister Dorothy Dawson and her daughter Denise Dawson for the first time. We immediately began to bond and get to know each other. I remember wishing I had gotten to know them sooner. From the very beginning, I felt their love for me, and I felt a strong family connection with them. Next was my brother Donald King Pledger. We hit it off immediately as well, back then I liked to drink and party, and so did Donald. We had some fun laughing, drinking, and just having a great time in each other's company. On one hand, I was sad about my father's passing, and on the other hand, I was so glad to meet and enjoy my newfound blood relatives.

The next few days were spent planning the funeral services for Mr. Pledge. We also went to my father's house and sorted through his personal effects for practical and personal reasons. That was a little hard for me to deal with, because I was able to get a better feel for who my father was, how he lived, and the things that were important to him. After we finished there, I needed a drink, so we picked up some rum and coke, and escaped from the reality of losing the man that was responsible for all of us being on the planet. The next day we all gathered at the Morning Star Baptist Church to lay our father to rest.

I have a vivid memory of only a few scenes at the home going service for my father. The first was the procession into the church where I was seated in the first two rows. The next thing I remember is an overwhelming feeling of heaviness and dread that overtook my emotions. I sat there feeling detached from the order of service, and even the reason why we were all there. Then suddenly, without warning or any pretense, I took in a deep breath and bolted out one of the side doors of the church and went running across the parking lot. When I finally came to a stop, I bent over and released a flood of emotions from way down deep. I was not grieving the past absence of my father, but I was releasing the pain of losing a future with my father that would never be. Today I look back on that moment as the crescendo of one of the greatest blessings of my life. God allowed me to meet and experience my father, to look into his eyes, hear his voice, enjoy his laugh, and listen to him talk about his God, who I didn't know then, but who is now my God too.

My father, Allen King Pledger, and his friend Ms. Isabel Jackson in Coral Gables, Florida

After laying our father to rest, I rode back to Chicago with my brother Donald and got a chance to meet many more of my extended Pledger family. I met the rest of Dorothy and Donald's children. I also met another sister named Marcia, who I adored at first sight. I remember how she would stare at me and widen her smile when our eyes connected. Marcia was a mother of four which included a daughter they called Danky, whose birth name is Cynthia, who I have gotten to know better over the years. Cynthia Williams is President of Austin Peoples Action Center, a vital social service agency serving Chicago's Austin Community and other communities in need of its services. I, along with Albert Featherstone recently had the pleasure of providing some Readiness Program Training to various groups of workforce trainees. I also met my younger brother, Tom Jordan (Pledger), who later came to California while serving in the U.S. Marines, at Camp Pendleton.

My Chicago family at a wedding reception for Birchie Williams, Jr., August 30, 1985. Dorothy is sitting in the front row, far left, Marcia is standing in the second row, far left, and my nieces, Cynthia, Denise, and Deborah, are standing in the third row.

As you can see, meeting my father opened the door to my big beautiful Chicago family who, over time, became connected to their California family. Unfortunately, my younger brother Tony and I have since lost a few siblings from our generation, James, Dorothy, Marcia, and Donald. I am now the oldest remaining son in the generation succeeding my father. I can truly say that the short time I was able to spend with my father has extended forty-four years beyond his death and has created family bonds that will last from generation to generation.

Health Restored

When I was running the streets of Oakland, I remember getting on a scale one day and I weighed 148 pounds, which made me about 35 pounds underweight. My hair was falling out in patches, due to a nervous condition brought on by excessive drug use and neglect of my health. I was developing an ulcer, my lungs were always congested, my skin was ruddy looking, and my eyes had dark circles around them. In short, I was a mess of a man and a menace to society. The truth was the cocaine was slowly killing me. Emotionally, I was a basket case, unable to concentrate or sit in one place for more than five minutes at a time.

As I have matured, I am much more mindful of my health and wellbeing. My addictive lifestyle was very taxing on my body. When you are on the go four to five days without sleep, not eating properly, drinking excessively daily, it will all come back to haunt you in the later years of your life. God's principle of sowing and reaping will prevail in every area of your life, especially when it comes to your health. Choosing to eat right, exercise, sleep properly and manage your stress will go a long way to offset what you will reap when it comes to living a dysfunctional life.

Once I made a conscious decision to change my life, all these areas began to improve. I now tip the scales at a solid 190 pounds, my nerves are calm, and I have inner peace. My eyes are clear and sharp, and I continue to get stronger each day. My relationship with the Lord is strong, and He has restored my self-respect and my willingness to live a life of social contribution.

Relationships Restored and Expanded

Life is about cultivating meaningful relationships with family, friends, co-workers, and people in general. As I look back on the many years I have lived on this earth, I can truly say that there has always been a direct relationship between my associations and the quality of my life. Even when I was not living right, I always managed to connect with people that added value to my life whether for good or evil. The truth is, while in my addiction, I managed to have fun, laugh, and even help others on many occasions.

One of "The Big Lies" I bought into was that "I was only hurting myself." The truth was my addiction impacted many significant relationships. Given enough time, addiction will destroy and weaken even the healthiest of relationships. At the lowest point of my downward spiral, all I cared about was how I would maintain my habit. It was all about me, myself, and I. That's the reason that when I became addicted, I separated myself from family, friends, business associates, and everyone who didn't feed my habit. I regret that I allowed my life to get so out of control.

Meeting my father opened the door to my big beautiful Chicago family

Only when I was able to clearly see myself for the

person I had become, was I able to come to terms with the reality of my selfish nature and dysfunctional lifestyle. On the night that I found myself on the hallway floor of my sister Margaret's house, I had come to the end of who I had become and was willing to surrender my addiction in exchange for a better life. The "Old Dwight" died that night on the floor, and the "New Dwight" stood up and walked in a manner consistent with my true purpose and destiny. It was a defining moment of change, and I would never be the same again. From that point forward, I began to build and cultivate many different and healthy relationships. Countless people have blessed my life in ways that I can't begin to describe. Yes, I am, happy, happy, happy!

Career Restored

In 1979, I traded my promising career as a real estate broker, co-owner and manager of an ongoing real estate firm, in exchange for a seven-year hiatus from reality as a drug addict, living a self-destructive life with no hope in sight. When I finally came to terms with the fact that I had to change and turn my life over to God, I never dreamed that I would ever sell real estate again. I had allowed my real estate broker's license to expire and even managed to get a felony conviction, which could potentially exclude me from ever working in the real estate profession again.

One day, while visiting my Aunt Clarine and Uncle Walter in Los Angeles, I stood with my uncle in their bedroom looking out the window at a construction project. He brought up the subject of real estate and asked if I had thought about getting back into it. Uncle Walter, a man I respected tremendously, began to encourage me to get my real estate license. He assured me that it would help me to get back on my feet. I took his words to heart, and I went back home and began studying for the state real estate exam. A few months later I went to San Diego, where the real estate exam was being administered. By the grace of God, I passed it and soon began selling real estate for Great Western Real Estate in Rialto, California.

I was so happy to be back in real estate. At that time the only transportation I had was an old yellow, 1975, Chevy LUV pick-up, with headlights that didn't work. But, I didn't let that stop me. Even though it meant I had to arrive home before dark, I wasn't bothered; I was just glad to be back in the game of life. And even with my raggedy truck, I was one of the top agents in the office. In my first year back, my production allowed me to receive a spot in the "Winners Circle," which is the second-highest award in the company. That was over thirty years ago, and since then I have been blessed to be in business for a total of forty-four years, having received my original license in 1975, the same year my Chevy truck rolled off the assembly line.

Divine Connections

Over the years, I have had the privilege of serving some amazing clients who have been a tremendous blessing to Sadie and me. One such client is a woman named Amy S. Harrison. I had the pleasure Amy meeting sixteen years ago through a letter of inquiry I wrote, requesting information on a piece of property she and her partner owned in Moreno Valley, California. After meeting Amy, I can truly say that my real estate business has never been the same. Since that first deal, I have represented Amy in many lucrative transactions. We have become close friends, which transcends the business aspect of our relationship. Sadie and I now manage Amy's many rental properties, along with other facets of her real estate portfolio.

Sadie with Amy Harrison at her annual SafeHouse Benefit Program at Victoria Gardens, Riverside, California in 2019.

As our relationship deepened beyond real estate, I found out that she not only owned multiple properties, but she is very active in philanthropic causes, such as Operation SafeHouse, which is a safe harbor for many homeless children and victims of human trafficking. Amy also operates a variety of businesses such as alternative schools for at-risk youth and students with special needs.

What I admire most about Amy is her compassionate heart for many of the people who rent from her. While managing Amy's properties, we have had situations in which the tenants have come upon hard times, such as job loss, a crippling illness, or other circumstances that impact their ability to pay their rent. I'm reminded of one such hardship case in which a tenant had been faithful in paying her rent, but after being diagnosed with cancer, she was no longer able to work. Once we verified the tenant's illness, Amy allowed her family to stay in the home for nearly a year, rent-free.

Just One Relationship

Another illustration of the value of just this one relationship happened around 2010 when the real estate market was in one of the worst economic downturns since the Great Depression. Property values were dropping 50% or more in some areas. Hundreds of real estate firms went under, and thousands of agents left the real estate business. At the same time, Sadie and I lost a rental property to foreclosure. We had put a large sum of money down on the property and took a $200,000 loss in purchase money and equity in the process.

Even though things were bad all around, we managed to maintain our primary home and pay our bills. It was largely due to Amy introducing me to a longtime friend of hers, Norman Brody, who over the next twelve months, paid cash for eight homes. After holding them for just over a year, Norman decided to liquidate his holdings, which meant eight listings and sales for me. One of those eight homes was sold to a lady I met named Wendy, a Taiwanese investor who purchased another five homes for cash. And it gets better because Wendy introduced me to her friend named Daniel, who over the next eighteen months purchased sixteen homes for cash, and two years later, decided to liquidate his inventory, and yes, that would mean 16 more listings and sales for me.

Just remember, all of this was the result of one letter of inquiry sent to Amy S. Harrison on September 2, 2004, and the rest is history. Equally as noteworthy is the fact that she knew about my troubled past and she still put a great deal of trust in me. Amy has literally purchased homes that she has never laid eyes on because of the trust that had developed between us. I value her not only as a client but also as a treasured friend. And, I share this story with you to illustrate how God will bring certain people into your life and give you favor with them. I think the biggest take away is that you should never underestimate the value of a single relationship that God may use to bless you for many years, and maybe even a lifetime. Amy Harrison is just one example of the many quality relationships I have been blessed to make in my real estate career. Of course, I thank God for all the key relationships that have helped to shape who I am today.

In the summer of 2004, I began to pursue motivational speaking and personal development training. It all began when Sadie and I were blessed to go on a Caribbean Cruise sponsored by Pastor T.D. Jakes of the Potter's House in Dallas. We had a great time relaxing, eating, and enjoying the different ports of call, and I hadn't been out to sea since my days in the Navy. They had some special guest celebrities on the cruise, and one such celebrity was the world-renowned motivational speaker, Mr. Les Brown. Since I had been speaking in churches, rehab centers, and even in prisons, I was looking forward to hearing what Les Brown had to say and hopefully meeting him.

> The "Old Dwight" died that night on the floor.

As Les was sharing his story of how he and his twin brother had been born on the floor of an abandoned building, I was captivated by his powerful speaking skills. Towards the end of his presentation, he introduced his daughter, Ona Brown, and another speaker named Art Doakes. Les was saying that he was beginning to train up-and-coming speakers to take over when he decides to retire. He also let the speakers share their success stories as professional speakers. I was impressed with the amount of money they were earning as speakers. Les then shared information about how someone could become a part of his Les Brown Speakers Network. Of course, I was very interested.

Platinum Speakers

The next morning, I was working out in the fitness room, and Art Doakes happened to be there as well. I went over and asked him a few questions about the Speakers Network. After chatting with Art, I spoke with Sadie and let her know that I was interested in joining Les Brown's program. She asked, "How much is it to join?" And when I said, "$5,000", she said, "What?!" I shared with her what Art said about the potential to earn money while making a positive impact on many lives as a professional speaker. Sadie gave me the green light, and I joined the Les Brown Speaker's Network, which later became known as the Les Brown Platinum Speaker Program.

Me with Les Brown at the Les Brown Speaker Network Training, Orlando, Florida, 2005.

After I returned home, someone from Les Brown's team, Valorie Parker-Hagen, contacted me. Valorie was the owner of a speaker-booking agency called Arise By VNP and was responsible for booking several professional speakers. Val, along with Lauren Hudson, a former TV personality, and speaker coach were tasked with getting me started in the Network. They were like my "speaker moms", introducing me to the speaker game. Since I had mainly spoken in church settings, sharing my Christian testimony, I had to learn how to speak without sounding so "preachy." I was very open to their guidance and direction. As I look back on my early association with Les Brown, I can truly say that if it had not been for Val and Lauren, I might not have been successful in making the transition from preachy to professional.

I remember the first speaker-training event I attended in Orlando, Florida at the Rosen Plaza Hotel. It was a very intimidating experience because I was surrounded by some very gifted speakers, like Johnny Wimbrey, Kevin Bracy, Dr. Charles Phillips, John Garcia, Johnny Morney Jr., Dr. Shirley Davis, Dr. Deavra Daughtry, Denise Young, Wade Randolph, Dan Smith, Art Doakes, Ona Brown, Alan McDougal, Donna Satchell Kimble, Stacie NC Grant, Breyon Burk, Chris Gloss, and Anita Hicks, just to name a few. We all represented the first wave of Platinum Speakers to be personally mentored and trained by Mr. Brown.

The It Factor

At that first event, we were all given five minutes to share our stories. I remember being very nervous when it was my turn to speak. For some reason, Les was not in the room when I shared my speech; I was hoping he would hear me speak. After sharing my addiction story, I received a standing ovation. Once I had finished, it seemed like everybody was coming over to congratulate me on my speech. The response from the other speakers made me feel welcome into the group and over time I became very close to some of the speakers. When Les finally came into the room, he was asking about how various speakers did. Once he made his way to me, he said someone told him I had the "It Factor." I didn't really know exactly what that meant, but I figured it was a good thing.

A few months later, I came to a second speaker training in Florida. This time I was able to get more acquainted with Les. I also met his mentor, Mike Williams, who is a phenomenal trainer and a great human being. Les and Mike were doing a sort of team training model, in which they would flow back and forth picking up on each other's content. It was at this training that I had an opportunity to speak in front of Les for the first time. It was just before the conclusion of the workshop, and Les asked Mike if he had ever heard me speak. Mike said, "No." Les then called me up to share my story. I had been working on my story since the previous workshop. I went right into my story, and when I concluded the story, I received a big applause. Les got a little emotional and told me that he wanted to continue working with me on my story. That was the beginning of what is now a 16-year relationship.

Never underestimate the value of a single relationship that God may use.

Through my relationship with Les, I have traveled and spoken in over 30 cities nationally and internationally. Les has been a huge factor in my development as a speaker, trainer, and coach. Even to this day, Les is one of my dearest friends on the planet. We are helpers to one another, in that he constantly encourages me in the area of speaker development, and I have been able to speak into his life on spiritual matters relating to his walk with God.

As I said earlier, I have made many strategic relationships through my association with Les, in much the same way I was able to do when I met Amy Harrison. Both came into my life providentially and for a greater purpose. A case in point is when I met a speaker named Dan Smith on a Cruise Your Way to Greatness event sponsored by Les Brown. Dan and his wife, Molly, were in the audience when I was doing a training piece for Les. After I spoke, Dan came over, introduced himself, purchased some of my products, and later signed up for one of my coaching programs.

D&D Training and Coaching Solutions

Over time, Dan and I became great friends. During a trip to the United Kingdom, we decided to start a speaking business that we later named D&D Training and Coaching Solutions. Dan and I have now been business partners for over ten years and have managed to become established in the speaking community as not only Les Brown Platinum Speakers, but also as accomplished trainers and coaches in our own right. We conduct periodic two-day, Three-Dimensional Speaker Training Workshops, as well as a Story Flow Model Coaching program that leads to certification as a 3D Speaker or Coach. We host weekly coaching calls, along with a new addition to our team, Tamara Williams. A talented speaker herself, Tamara adds tremendous value to our team. She is a great support to Dan and me because she understands our nuanced teaching style. Dan and I are looking forward to leaving our indelible "footprint" in the speaking community.

I never cease to be amazed by the possibilities stemming from relationships we encounter that literally change the course and destiny of our lives. It's been said that your success could be just one relationship away. This reminds me of a dear friend I met through my association with Les Brown, Deavra A. Daughtry. Hailing from Houston, she is the president and CEO of Excellent Care Management and Excel E. Care, one of the largest personal in-home care agencies in the country. Deavra has hired and trained over 10,000 in-home care workers since launching her business. She is also the founder of the Texas Women's Empowerment Foundation (TWEF).

Deavra, who is also a first-generation Les Brown Platinum Speaker, attended the second Speaker Training in Orlando. Before I was introduced to Deavra through a mutual friend, the late Dr. Charles Phillips, I noticed that during the two-day training Deavra would sit in on a portion of the workshop and be absent from other parts of the training. I remember thinking, "She's not getting her money's worth out of the training." Deavra didn't speak very much, and I wondered what her story was because everyone has a story.

On the second day of the workshop, I found out that Deavra indeed had a very compelling story. She shared about how as a single parent of two, unemployed, and in need of clear direction, she decided to do all she could with what she had, from where she was in life. With her grandmother as her first in-home care client, Deavra started Excel E. Care out of the trunk of her car. With her well-worn leather briefcase for a file cabinet, Deavra began what would later become a successful multi-million-dollar enterprise.

Our friend Deavra Daughtry, with son Chazsten H. Daughtry and Ebone Stowers. Houston, Texas.

The Rock and The Rose

Deavra had heard me share my story several times and thought my story would add value to her next community event. The topic would be on relationships. What made this event special is that it would be the first time I would share my story, and refer to my wife Sadie as, "My Rose." My talk was titled, "The Enduring Love of The Rock and The Rose." The room was packed out, and as I stood on the stage sharing my story, I came to the place in the story where my wife Sadie was picking me up at the airport, after an over five-year separation. I remember saying, "She came around that corner in an old Chevy Nova car," and then I said, "She should have done a drive-by. But she didn't do a drive-by, because when she could have chosen hate, she chose love, and when she could have chosen revenge, she chose to forgive. It's been said that forgiveness is like the sweet fragrance that a rose leaves on the foot that crushed it!"

As I was saying the last part, I dropped a fresh red rose on the stage, picked my foot up, and crushed it. As I stamped my foot on the rose, the crowd seemed to gasp, and then I leaned over and picked up the crushed rose. Since that night in Houston, I have included that forgiveness quote, in the telling of my story, always mentioning the "sweet fragrance of the rose," after it had been crushed.

Attending her event in Houston was the beginning of a long-time friendship with Deavra, her two children, Chaz and Ebone, and the many other relationships that spun from our association. Since that first time, I have made many trips back to Houston to speak, preach, and conduct speaker training workshops, staff development seminars, and executive coaching.

Purpose and Potential

My friendship with Deavra led me to another powerful and influential thought leader, the late Dr. Myles Munroe. Dr. Munroe was a trusted mentor to Deavra and served as a father figure who saw her as a "daughter of purpose." Deavra has even titled one of her books, *From Purpose to Blessing*. I remember riding with him on a hotel tram that was transporting us to an event venue in downtown Houston. We met and had a brief conversation. I let him know that I often shared his quote about the wealthiest place on the planet. He chuckled a bit and even seemed to be humbled by my complimentary admission.

This is Dr. Munroe's quote that I love to share, "The wealthiest place on the planet is not in the vast oil fields of the Middle East, nor is it in the gold and diamond mines of South Africa. The wealthiest place on the planet is the graveyard, for there you will find dreams that were never realized, books that were never written, gifts, talents, and abilities that never reached their full potential. Men and women who lived and died with their greatness still in them." As you think about Dr. Munroe's quote, consider the following question. If you died today, what would die with you, what gift, talent or ability would you go with you to your grave?

As a minister, I've had the opportunity to officiate and eulogize many people over the years, and when we end up at the deceased's final resting place, the graveyard, I share Dr. Munroe's quote with those who are present. I also bring their attention to the many grave-stones and markers throughout the cemetery. I tell them that what makes the graveyard a wealthy place is the unused potential and talents that many took with them to their grave. I also remind them that we can't do anything about the unused potential taken to the grave, but we can do something with the unused potential in each one of us. We can decide that whatever gift or talent we have, we are going to deposit it on the earth and not in the earth. In other words, we will choose to "Live full and die empty."

I remember sharing that quote with a dear friend named Marie Cathrie Dukes. She heard me share it at a memorial service for a mutual friend named Curtis Bonaparte, Sr. who we both knew from church. About six months later Marie enlisted my services to help with a manuscript she wanted to be published. I was very excited because I had been telling her for several years that she had a book in her. What she told me next really blessed me. She said, "When I heard you share that quote at Curtis Bonaparte's memorial service, I went home and started working on my book." I agreed to help her organize her chapters, and work with her story content and story flow. About six months later Marie published a 299-page autobiography titled, *from riches to TRUE RICHES*. It should be noted that Marie was in her late sixties when she managed to get that book out of her and into the minds and hearts of the many who will be blessed and encouraged by her story.

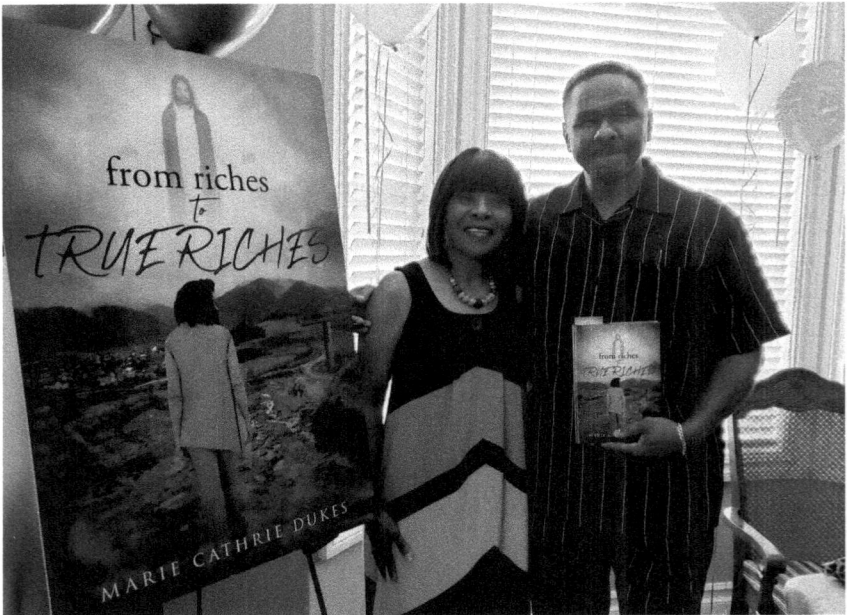

Dwight with friend and author, Marie Dukes, at a book signing in her beautiful home in Riverside, California.

One of the key components of my restoration and recovery journey has been the many relationships I have been blessed with. Recovery doesn't take place in a vacuum but in the context of nurturing and healthy relationships that add value and meaning to your life. All of the relationships discussed in this section did not come about because of luck or coincidence, but I believe they were brought about by divine providence. My constant prayer is that God would order my steps and that He would lead and guide in the way He would have me to go.

Possessions Restored

I began this book by painting a "before" picture of my life. I listed some of the material possessions I had acquired, which included two well-furnished homes, four cars, two of which were Mercedes Benz. I also let you know that when I came to the end of my seven-year addiction, I had lost everything, even down to just the clothes on my back. When I came back to my wife and children, I found them living in a very old, two-bedroom rental house, and driving a 1974 Chevy Nova, which of course added to the guilt I was experiencing. I can also say that even though it was a humble dwelling, there was more authentic love in that home than was ever in our big 4-bedroom, 3-bathroom home in San Diego. It's the strength of the love mutually shared by the people that makes a home and not the material things that take up space in the home.

The good news is that in a relatively short amount of time, we were blessed to purchase and move into our own home. Since I returned home, we have moved no less than seven times in the last thirty years and each time moving into a better neighborhood and a larger home. We have also managed to acquire better cars, home furnishing, and have been able to live a comfortable lifestyle. All of our children had an opportunity to attend college and have gone on to excel in their respective life pursuits. At the top of the list of what has been added to our lives over the years are our seven grandchildren, who have added a dimension to our lives that words cannot explain. Even with the occasional drama, the good times have far outweighed the bad times.

Looking back, I remember when I was being counseled by Pastor Hubbard, and I told him that I didn't care about getting back any of the material things that had been lost due to my addiction; all I wanted was to be free from drugs and have peace of mind. He told me that God would restore all that I once had and even give me more. Pastor Hubbard has since passed away, but the words he spoke to me when I was still dealing with the consequences of my poor life choices have literally come to pass in my life. God has far exceeded all my expectations. Along with what He has allowed me to own, He has also given me a peace that surpasses all understanding, and for that, I am eternally grateful.

> *All of our children had an opportunity to attend college and have gone on to excel.*

Yes, God has truly been good to me. In short, I cannot begin to tell you how liberating it feels to be free from the bondage of a crack addiction that destroyed my life. There is not a day that goes by that I don't look back and take note of where I was and immediately begin to appreciate how far the Lord has brought me.

In the more than thirty years I have been on this path of restoration, Sadie and I have not only acquired many of the material possessions we lost, but we have been able to enjoy the process together, one challenge at a time. As I said before, prior to giving my life to the Lord, I took credit for any tangible possessions I had acquired. I thought it was because of my hard work and my intelligence that I was able to achieve the "stuff." I have since found out that it is God Who gives us the power to gain wealth. So, I acknowledge Him for all that I have been blessed with. If restoration is to take place in a person's life, they must realize that they will have to change from their way to God's way. I proved what I could do with a life when I was in charge. I'm so glad that I was given a second chance to get it right and to do it God's way, which is the best way.

Restoration Ministries

In the days, weeks, and years after getting up off the floor at Margaret's house in 1986, I took on a whole new mindset. Now that I was clean and sober, I developed a burning desire to do what I could to help other strug-gling addicts to get free from their addictions. My heart also went out to the many family members who were still

I have made many strategic relationships through my association with Les.

struggling with their addictions. The truth is that for every addict, multiple relationships are negatively affected. The collateral damage done cannot even be calculated when it comes to the many people who have been harmed by the behavior of just one addict in the family, not to mention the impact on future generations to come who will pattern their lives after a father, mother or relative's addictive behavior.

It's been over thirty years since my journey of recovery began, but I am still dealing with the fallout from that one moment of weakness in my friend's kitchen. It was clearly a defining moment that changed the course and destiny of my life.

Early on in my Christian experience, I got involved in a restoration support group. If my recovery was to be successful, I had to connect myself to a supportive group of people who could not only relate to what I was going through but would also be a safe place to work through my, addiction-related, post-traumatic stress. I remember attending meetings in Grand Terrace, California, where a husband and wife couple, Cliff and Freddie Harris, facilitated the sessions. They later founded the Drug Alternative Program (DAP), an ongoing, very successful, Christ-centered, in-house drug treatment program in California and Alabama.

Cliff and Freddie Harris, Founders of Drug Alternative Program, in 2008.

The weekly group sessions included a time of topical teaching, followed by an open discussion, and concluded with a time of prayer and personal ministry. These sessions gave me time to reflect on my ordeal with drugs and alcohol, while also allowing me to hear other addicts and codependents share their stories. Since attending those meetings in Grand Terrace, I have continued to be connected to an ongoing support group ministry. My friend, the late, Evangelist Doreen Thornton, was known for saying that, "recovery is a lifestyle," and I wholeheartedly agree with her.

After attending Cliff and Freddie's DAP support group, and picking up the model, I had a conversation with Pastor Hubbard about starting a restoration support group at Community Baptist Church. When I met with Pastor Hubbard and shared my vision for the support group, he permitted us to hold a weekly Friday night meeting at the church.

> *If you died today what gift, talent or ability would go with you to your grave?*

On May 5, 1989, the restoration support ministry met for the first time. This group would be the beginning of my journey of working with other struggling addicts and their families. My co-leaders were my prayer partners, Deacon Elrie Stuart, and my sister, Rev. Margaret Winn. In the succeeding years, we saw God transform many lives through our restoration support group. We later helped other ministries to start restoration support groups at their churches.

Community Baptist Restoration Support Ministry, 1st Annual Celebration of Freedom, Redlands, California, in 1990.

Ray of Hope

As I became stronger, I co-founded a 501(c)3 non-profit with Elder Greg D. Williams. We named it, Ray of Hope Ministries, which was a para-church ministry supporting churches, prisons, rehab centers, and other non-profit organizations. Through Ray of Hope, my longtime friend, Greg D. Williams, along with our wives, Sadie and Cassandra Williams, led a team of former drug addicts and alcoholics, such as Pastor Albert Featherstone, Elder Pat Lewis, Evangelist Sandra Thomas, Pastor Brad Comer, Minister Mary Love Comer, Pastor James Miller, Evangelist Nedra Campbell-Downs, Pastor Johnny Taylor, Elder Cassandra Walker, and many others. We even had board members who had never used drugs but wanted to support the vision of Ray of Hope Ministries. People like Skip Showalter, a Riverside police officer, and his wife Joanna, along with Rev. Don and Beverly Slack, assisted with carrying out the mission.

Ray of Hope Ministries Board of Directors and faithful supporters, taken at our Annual Restoration Conference, Moreno Valley, California, 1998.

Armed with our testimonies of how God had changed our lives, we managed to bring hope and spiritual healing to countless addicts, and to those who love them. We were blessed to share our stories in parks, on street corners, in churches, prisons, and wherever there were men and women trapped by addiction or social malady. Over the years we were able to witness the deliverance and restoration of many hundreds of men and women, who had destroyed their lives and ruined the lives of people close to them. We managed to open a recovery support facility called the Center of Hope, in San Bernardino, California.

*Ray of Hope Ministries, Center of Hope in San Bernardino,
California, the birthplace of two churches, in 1993.*

The accomplishment we are most thankful to God for is our ability
to successfully open and operate two recovery homes for women,
one of which housed women with children. We named the main
house, Magdalene Manor, a reference to Mary Magdalene in the
Bible.

Magdalene Manor, San Bernardino, California, in 1993.

It was incredibly challenging to keep up with the demands of running both homes. Somehow, we always managed to get what we needed to continue helping the residents and their children. When I think of many women who resided at Magdalene Manor, one story that comes to mind is that of a young lady named Shannon Rabb, who came to the home eight months pregnant. She was traumatized by a past of prostitution, domestic violence, and being buried alive and left for dead. Shannon had recently arrived in California where her drug activity and prostitution continued until her aunt brought her to Magdalene Manor.

Shortly after coming into the home, Shannon gave birth to a beautiful baby girl she named Shanice Chelsea Rabb, but we called her "Baby Hope." Shannon really loved her daughter, and seemed to be more serious about her recovery, because she wanted to one day have her own place to raise her child. Chelsea, as Shannon liked to refer to her as, really brought life to the home, and all the sisters helped Shannon take care of her little girl. Having her in the home was a source of inspiration and encouragement to me as well.

When Chelsea was about five and a half months old, she became very ill and passed away. As expected, Shannon took her daughter's passing very hard and grieved on a deep level. We were all heart-broken when she passed away. I feared that Chelsea's passing would cause Shannon to relapse. Thankfully, Shannon stayed with the program and prepared to give Chelsea a worthy home going celebration. With all that I was going through to keep the homes going, seeing and holding Chelsea was a much-needed breath of fresh air.

Shannon Rabb and her little princess, Shanice Chelsea Rabb, also known as "Baby Hope," San Bernardino, California 1993.

God provided everything needed for the funeral service. Chelsea was laid to rest in a small custom size casket. Chelsea looked like a little doll, with a beautiful white dress and bonnet on her head. It would be the first funeral service in the Center of Hope, which was located directly across the street from Magdalene Manor. I remember Chelsea's service being very difficult to officiate because I had become very attached to her. Many people heard about what happened and attended Chelsea's memorial service. It was a very emotional and moving service with many tears of sorrow shed. Chelsea's casket was small enough to be placed in the back seat of one of the mourner's car, and transported to the Green Acres Cemetery, in Bloomington, California.

Understandably, Shannon was heartbroken and grieved Chelsea's passing deeply. Losing her daughter seemed to take the wind out of Shannon's desire for recovery. She became depressed and wanted to give up on her recovery, even despairing of life itself. One day I came into the women's home, walked by Shannon's bedroom, and found her cutting her wrist with a razor blade while crying uncontrollably. I entered the room and grabbed her arm, held her, and prayed until the paramedics arrived to transport her to the hospital.

I must admit that I became discouraged after that incident. I really wanted Shannon to turn her life around for the better, but she had to want it more than me. Shortly after that incident, Shannon left the women's home and moved back to Las Vegas, where she had grown up. Ultimately, the financial and emotional responsibility of operating two recovery homes took its toll, and the Ray of Hope Board of Directors decided to close the homes.

The Grace of God

I lost track of Shannon for many years, until one day, I was on Facebook and ran across a post with the name, Shannon Rabb. I immediately clicked on the name and was taken to her Facebook profile picture. I was very happy to see that Shannon was not only still alive but thriving. We later connected and Shannon filled in the blanks of her life's journey since leaving the recovery home. She had temporarily relapsed and returned to her old life on the streets of Las Vegas; that decision landed her back in the penitentiary three more times. Fortunately, she was able to get clean and sober and begin to live a productive life. Shannon also let me know that she was gainfully employed and had recently received an award for Employee of the Month.

Sadie and I eventually went to Las Vegas and visited Shannon at her place of employment. Shannon gave us a tour of her workspace. We met many of her co-workers who said that Shannon was a blessing to work with every day. We had a great lunch and enjoyed our time catching up. You can't imagine the joy that flooded my heart knowing that Shannon had finally gotten her life together.

Shannon is an example of why we can't stop doing all we can to help those who have lost their way. You never know when they will see the light and all of your labor will not have been in vain. We must keep planting those seeds of hope, and God will give the increase at the appointed time. Shannon and I stay in touch via Facebook or on the phone, and ever-present in my mind is the miracle of the grace of God in Shannon's life.

Pastor Ray Hahn presenting me with the Dove Award
in Moreno Valley, California. 2008

Youth on Fire

After closing the home, we later moved to Moreno Valley, California. I took a position as a Youth Pastor for Moreno Valley Christian Fellowship (MVCF), under the leadership of Pastor Ray Hahn. I met Pastor Hahn through a mutual friend who pastored Friendship Christian Fellowship, Pastor Art Wooten, who had given Pastor Hahn one of my books to read. After reading my book, Pastor Hahn said he read it from cover to cover, and with tears in his eyes, got down on his knees and thanked God for my transformed life. He later told Pastor Wooten that he wanted to meet me. When we met, Pastor Hahn asked me to join his leadership team. In the seven years that I served at MVCF, I was blessed to get a taste of full-time ministry, receive a decent salary with benefits, and have an opportunity to minister to hundreds of God's people.

While serving as Youth Pastor, I experienced some of the most rewarding and memorable moments of my entire time in ministry. We named our ministry Youth on Fire (for God), and witnessed God do some amazing things in the life of his young people. This ministry allowed me to serve with some phenomenal youth leaders, who had hearts for serving and mentoring the next generation of servant leaders.

I was especially blessed to serve with a very unlikely youth minister named Skip Showalter. I say unlikely because Skip just happened to be a police officer with the Riverside Police Department. Our working together proves that God has a sense of humor because for many years I spent much of my time running from and avoiding the police. Initially Skip and I had some growing pains, but we soon moved past our differences and became close friends doing God's work.

Me with Skip Showalter and Rev. Don Slack for Skip's promotion to Sergeant, Riverside, California, December 2002. Skip was later promoted to Lieutenant in June 2014.

Skip later became a part of Ray of Hope Ministries, and soon began to accompany me into prison and youth rehabilitation centers. Skip also invited one of his fellow police officers named Ken Tutwiler to a prison outreach. Ken eventually became more involved in prison ministry, and later established his own outreach ministry called, "Cops Out Preaching Salvation" (COPS). They now take teams of law enforcement officers into prisons across the nation preaching and teaching the love of God to inmates and correctional officers who are in earshot. Our friendship was a clear example of how God can match the unlikeliest of people to do a mighty work for Him. Our families have shared some very memorable moments, and I thank God for bringing the Skip and Joanna Showalter into my life.

After a few years, I was later elevated to the position of Associate Pastor, and that's when my ministry focus went to another level. I watched God transform our ministry into one of the most ethnically diverse congregations in Moreno Valley. Our Praise and Worship ministry was second to none when it came to stirring up the manifest presence of God. We would go from high praise to tearful and intimate worship of our God. Pastor Hahn was very open to the diverse make-up of the church, even though some were not of the same mindset. It was clear that God was doing a special work in our church, and it was marvelous in our eyes.

Just as God did with the Youth Ministry, He also showed Himself mighty in the church as a whole. I was blessed to do some of the Sunday morning preachings, along with teaching Wednesday night Bible Study. In early 2000, my season at MVCF came to an end. I look back on the seven years at MVCF and thank God for my friend Pastor Ray Hahn, and all the beautiful people that I had the privilege of serving and being blessed by. Reflecting on the past thirty years of ministry, I believe the single most important factor that has allowed me, and others to get and remain drug-free, is being a part of an ongoing support system, which included a weekly restoration support group.

Solutions Ministry

Even at this writing, I can say that I still attend a support ministry at my current home church, CrossWord Christian Church in Moreno Valley, California, where Bishop L. Kirk Sykes is the Senior Pastor. Shortly after joining CrossWord Church, Minister Sheldon Henderson and I met with Bishop Sykes and let him know that we were available to start a restoration ministry at CrossWord if that was part of his vision.

After committing it to prayer, Bishop Sykes released us to co-lead the Solutions 4 L.I.F.E. restoration ministry at CrossWord, along with Sister Shelly Robinson. The scope of the ministry would go beyond just drug and alcohol addiction and include people who are struggling with any number of "issues" that hinder them from living a life of freedom and purpose.

Me with Bishop L. Kirk Sykes and Minister Sheldon Henderson at CrossWord Church, Riverside, California, 2019 where we conducted a small group facilitator training.

For the past eight years, our Solutions Ministry has conducted a 12-week book study titled, *Making Peace with Your Past*: *Help for Adult Children of Dysfunctional Families.* The author, Tim Sledge, taps into the impact and fallout from growing up in a dysfunctional family, and how it can cause any number of personality and behavior problems in a person's life. I have attended and facilitated the Making Peace groups and have witnessed many amazing transformations in the lives of the attendees. I highly recommend this 12-week study for any ministry or organization that focuses on transforming lives in a real and lasting way.

The Prodigal Son

There was one particular Bible story that was instrumental in helping me to see how the love of God worked in my life, and how my story was very similar to the story of this younger son. The story found in Luke Chapter 15, talks about a father who had two sons, and how the younger son went to his father and asked for his inheritance early. After the father granted his request, he went into a country far away, and there he wasted away his inheritance in riotous and loose living. After he had lost everything he owned, he became hungry, but no one would give him anything to eat. When the boy finally came to himself, he returned from the far country, and after asking his father to forgive him, the Bible says, "But the father said to his servants, bring forth the best robe and put it on him, and put a ring on his hand, and shoes on his feet, and bring the fatted calf, and kill it, and let us eat and be merry; for this my son was dead and is alive again; he was lost, but is found, and they began to be merry."

When I heard that story, I remember thinking that the son's story was my story. Just like that son, I had been restored in many areas of my life, and there is a joy down on the inside of me that words cannot explain. It all began when I asked God to take full control of my life. Jesus not only took control, but He also gave me peace of mind, a clear conscience, and a desire to be all that I could be for Him.

The incredible truth is that when it comes to restoration, no matter how bad a person has ruined their life, redemption is possible. I have witnessed countless numbers of people who after making a total mess of their lives were able to rebuild their self-respect and character. My story is one of the many thousands who are living examples of what's possible for anyone who truly desires to be restored. Always remember that what's possible for one, is possible for all. The choice is yours!

——— *Fifteen* ———

Sadie Speaks

A s you know I have been sharing my story of addiction, redemption, and restoration, nationally and internationally. The following story consists of excerpts from a pre-recorded one-on-one video interview of Sadie. In this interview, conducted by the renowned motivational speaker, Mr. Les Brown, Sadie breaks her silence and shares from the heart of a woman, the devastating impact that my addiction had on her life, and how she was able to pick up the pieces and make a life for herself and our two children during my five and a half year absence. Sadie's story is one of the power of forgiveness, healing, and the ultimate restoration of our once fragmented relationship. It begins with Sadie picking up the pieces after we lost our home in San Diego:

> When it was clear that we were losing our home in San Diego, I remember scraping up some pennies and coins, loading up the kids, some belongings, and going to the gas station. We ran out of gas right in front of the station. After getting some help, I used the coins to buy gas and headed to my mother-in-law's home in Redlands, California. Shortly after moving in with her, she decided to move

to Arkansas, so we were faced with having to move again. I realized that going to stay with my mother was not an option, because there were still some unresolved issues with my stepfather, and I was not going to introduce my children to that situation. I settled on moving in with my sister and her husband.

The first thing on my agenda was to get a job, but in the process of doing so, my car broke down. With no car, I had to turn to public transportation. Yes, I had to catch the bus. I would start my day early in the morning and I would end it late in the evening. I eventually ended up with not one, but two jobs. The first was at Sierra Savings where I worked an 8:00 A.M. to 5:00 P.M. shift. The second was at a small janitorial company, that had me working all hours of the night and it required me to catch the bus late at night. I desperately needed my life to take on some sense of normalcy again, so I could begin to provide my children with a stable environment.

While in transition, I moved in with my sister and brother-in-law, who lived in San Bernardino, California. After a while, I began to receive calls from Dwight. He wanted to come and see the kids and me. His visits became more frequent. He would come to get me and we would go to a local motel. Even when we would go to the motel, I was not alone with him, because he would do his drugs while we were together.

After a while, my brother-in-law was fed up. He told me that Dwight was treating me like a prostitute. Dwight came into town, took me to a motel, and brought me back again. He said, "It's a continuous cycle with no end in sight. At some point, you have to realize what you are doing to yourself and the children." After talking to my brother-in-law, I knew I had to put an end to it. So, I told Dwight I could no longer go to the motel with him. He needed to take some steps to change his life.

After several months, I got a call from Dwight. He told me that he had re-enlisted in the Navy. He wanted me to come and be with him. I asked him if he was going to be able to provide for me and the children. He said that I would have to get a job. When he said that, I realized he still did not have any answers for me. There was no job for me, and that was no place to raise my children. I decided to continue staying with my sister until he figured things out. I did agree to send our furniture to him in Oakland, California.

While separated from Dwight, I made a decision not to get involved in another relationship. I didn't want to expose my children to different men going in and out of their lives. I chose to put that part of my life on hold until my children became of age.

One weekend I took the kids to see Dwight in Oakland. My sister and brother-in-law also went along with me. I still remember going up to this small apartment door. When I knocked, a fair-skinned woman with long hair answered the door. She had a baby in her arms. She let us in and disappeared up the stairs. Shortly afterward, Dwight came down.

Dwight acted like there was nothing wrong. He sat down in the chair next to me. I began to look around the apartment, and it's my furniture, it's my wall hangings, it's my mirrors, and it's my clocks on the walls. I was thinking, "That's my television," and what went through my mind is, all I want to do is go over there and put my foot through that T.V. I had to keep telling myself, "But that's not you; that is the anger inside of you." I also couldn't understand why no one told me about the baby! We didn't stay long. I was so upset that I forgot to leave the kids' clothes. I just headed straight to the car.

As we were driving back to Southern California, my sister kept saying, "Did you see that woman; she looked like you." How could I not see her? I really didn't pay attention to her; all I saw was the baby. I could not wait to get back home. The first thing I did was call Dwight. I waited patiently for him to answer. When I first heard his voice, I asked about the baby. He responded, "Well, Sadie, you know it just happened." I continued, "Why didn't you tell me?" As always, Dwight was persistent. He continued, "It happened and I just didn't want to tell you." He went on to say, "I've always told you to go on with your life."

Shortly after getting back home, I got sick. I started having massive migraine headaches, my eyes were bloodshot, and

I was totally stressed out. I started having a reoccurring dream that Dwight had died. I just kept having the same dream repeatedly. In my dream, someone from the military would bring me a letter stating that Dwight was dead.

During this time, I had lost contact with Dwight. I didn't have a phone number that worked. All I could do was hope he would contact me. I knew I could not continue going on feeling the way I was feeling. I realized no matter what, I had to forgive him. Not for what it was going to do for him, but for what it would do for me. Forgiving him was going to set me free... and I needed to be free.

I realized that if anything happened to him, and I had not forgiven him, I would not be able to live with myself. Finally, the phone rang, and it was Dwight. The first thing out of my mouth was, "Dwight, I forgive you." I said, "Part of this is my fault because when you asked me to come live with you, I could have come, but I chose not to." So, it wasn't totally all his fault.

At some point in our lives, we have to say those words to someone who has done us wrong, "I forgive you." Forgiveness is the true freedom of the soul. I know that if I was ever going to be with Dwight, I had to forgive him, and I had to leave the things he had done in the past. There was no way our relationship would work if I were constantly bringing up the past to him.

Even today, when I run across young people that are having problems and they are talking about getting divorced, I discuss forgiveness with them. I let them know if they take their spouse back, they have to put the past behind them, or they will be miserable. Really, forgiveness is about you and not the other person.

If I focused on what Dwight did to me, it caused me physical and emotional pain. When I began to forgive him, God allowed me to forgive myself. For the most part, keeping him captive kept me captive too. When things go wrong, no one walks away faultless. I was haunted by the decisions I had made. I realized that I could have done things differently as well. My forgiveness gave him freedom and it gave me freedom as well.

About five and a half years into our separation, I got a call at work from Dwight's sister Margaret. She said, "Dwight wants to come back home." I said, "No, he wants to come back home to you or one of his other sisters. Why can't he stay with one of you?" She said, "No, he wants to come home to you." I finally said, "Yes, he can come to my house."

The next day I got a call from Margaret, letting me know that Dwight was waiting at Ontario Airport. My first thought was, "What am I going to do?" I was working at Great Western Bank at the time, so I asked my assistant manager what she thought I should do. She immediately said, "Go pick him up! Go get him!"

Dwight had been in jail for a short time, and I still wasn't sure what I was in for or who would be waiting for me. Would I finally be picking up Dwight, the man I married, or would this be the man life had allowed him to become? I had a small two-bedroom masonry house, which would be enough space for us. It was very comfortable for my two children and me. On the way to the airport, I kept playing things out in my mind. I thought he could stay in my room and I would stay in the kids' room. We would be together – and not together if you know what I mean. Alternatively, I found myself thinking about making breakfast for him and picking up where we left off.

Finally, I turned the corner at the airport. After all this time, there he was, standing on the curbside. He was much thinner than I had seen him before he had gotten so far into drugs. My first thoughts were that he had let his hair grow out, and his clothes really weren't matching or what I would call matching.

When he got in the car, I nervously smiled at him and he smiled back. He leaned over and kissed me as if no time had passed by – and we drove off.

The next morning, I brought him breakfast in bed. I was accustomed to doing that before he left, and I was accustomed to making the children's breakfast every morning, so it was no different that morning either.

Soon I realized that even though Dwight didn't bring the drugs in our house, he did bring foul language and alcohol with him. I had to let him know our lives had been peaceful and the children weren't used to that kind of language. I could not allow him to destroy the peace the children

had become accustomed to having. He didn't fight with me over this issue. He respected my decision.

Although I had never gone into any details about Dwight with the kids while he was gone, they did miss him. Once he came back, my daughter, Michelle would not let him out of her sight. She followed him around everywhere he went. It was evident she did not want to lose her father again.

Just as quickly as our lives had taken a turn for the worst, they took a turn for the better. Dwight finally got clean. Believe it or not, that was a hard thing for me to deal with. His sober side was just as extreme as his addicted side. Sometimes people tend to go overboard. Once Dwight straightened up, he wanted to change the whole world.

Dwight found the Lord. He gave up drugs, but the church became his new drug of choice. It was like he was still addicted. His entire life revolved around nothing but the Lord. So, for the children and me, he was still in a sense addicted. He was just addicted to something else. Even though Dwight was at home now, it was as if he still hadn't come back to his family. He spent most of his time help-ing all those that were on drugs or in recovery. He was at the church almost every day of the week. As far as I was concerned, he was still on drugs.

Now when Dwight talks about restoration, he says that it has been a long road, the truth is, it has been a long hard road. I will say that it has been worth it. Dwight had to find a balance in his life. He had to find the balance that included God, his wife, *and* his family.

I still remember my wedding vows to Dwight. My vows stated, "For better or worse." I never dreamed how bad the worse would be or how good the better would be. I realize through the years that God has allowed our challenges to lead us to our purpose. No matter what has happened, there has always been something to keep us connected to the Lord. At this point, I can truly put the past behind us, and realize the best is yet to come.

After Les Brown completed the interview with Sadie, he asked me to come and view what they had recorded. I remember sitting next to Sadie watching the interview and listening to her story. Sadie shared things that I was hearing for the very first time. The more she shared the more I could feel emotions stirring deep inside. When she came to the part about coming to Oakland and learning that I had fathered a child. I literally broke down and cried as she was explaining how it affected her health and mental state.

> *True forgiveness cancels out all excuses for withholding love.*

I had no idea that she had gone through something like that. As she said in the video, she couldn't understand why no one had told her about Latoya.

The blessing is that after returning home from Northern California and being reunited with her and our children. She consented to let Latoya spend the summer with us in Southern California, and

Sadie treated Latoya as one of her own children. Latoya came to live with us permanently at age 13. Sadie has always felt that Latoya should not have to suffer for a situation that she had no control over.

Most women aren't as open to allowing a child from an extra-marital affair to be a part of their father's life, and certainly not open to that child moving into their home. I think it's a credit to both Sadie and Yvette for being willing to do what they thought was best for Latoya at the time. Later when Latoya graduated from high school, Yvette and her husband came to our home in Moreno Valley to attend the graduation and show support to Latoya.

To Forgive Divine

Over the years when I have told my story in various cities across America, and when I share things about the kind of person Sadie is, they marvel at her forgiving nature. Not only because of how she accepted me back after I had been so unfaithful, but also her atti-tude towards Latoya and her mother Yvette. Sadie's tough love and forgiveness made it possible for me to put forth the effort to stay clean and sober for over thirty years. If it had been any other way, I'm not sure I would be telling this same story. Her forgiveness was nothing short of miraculous.

I define a miracle as something that's not supposed to happen in the normal course of life. I put the phenomena called "forgiveness" in that category because it's not a natural or normal occurrence that just happens in a vacuum. The thing that makes it a miracle is the spiritual and emotional freedom experienced by the forgiver and the release of the forgiven. It's a conscious intentional act of the will. The power of forgiveness is a mystery yet to be fully understood by mere mortals. I say that because when forgiveness is fully rendered and received, it changes something in the chemistry of a person's mind, emotions, and will. That's why it's been said, "To err is human, to forgive divine." I agree with my friend Dr. Ona Brown who said, "True forgiveness cancels out all excuses for withholding love." We are most like God when we forgive from our hearts.

Having said that, I want to share an experience that occurred at the passing of one of my best friends, Greg D. Williams. He and I were victims of the worst drug epidemics to hit America in modern times. As I shared earlier in my story, we both were eventually set free from our addictions and began serving the Lord and living clean and sober lives. My friend Greg made his transition to heaven on September 2, 2017, and was laid to rest on September 16, 2017, in Richmond, California.

Sadie and I traveled up to Richmond for Greg's Celebration of Life. I was asked by his wife Cassandra to give the eulogy, which I did with mixed emotions. On the one hand, I was glad that my friend did not have to suffer any longer from his multiple illnesses, and on the other hand, I was already missing my friend.

> We were victims of the worst drug epidemics to hit America in modern times.

The service went well, with many expressions of gratitude for the impact he had on the lives of many in attendance. Greg lived a life of service and social contribution. I experienced a great deal of empathy for his grieving wife and their children who would miss Greg tremendously.

The late Pastor Greg D. Williams after being presented with his Dove Award for 20 or more years clean and sober, Moreno Valley, California, 2008.

After laying Greg to rest at a nearby cemetery, Sadie and I returned to our hotel room to relax. While there I received a text message from Yvette, expressing why she was unable to attend Greg's funeral. I let Sadie know that I had received the text from Yvette and informed her that I was going to send a reply. I responded to her text, and then I received another text from Yvette in which she communicated her desire to ask Sadie to forgive her for what happened in the past.

Due to the sensitive nature of that subject matter, I was somewhat nervous about relaying the message to Sadie. After sharing Yvette's text with Sadie, I asked her how she wanted me to respond to the text. Without hesitation, Sadie told me to let Yvette know that she had already forgiven her. By now it was clear that we were experiencing a defining moment of forgiveness.

Before replying to Yvette's text, I let Sadie know that I would also be asking Yvette to forgive me for our past as well. Sadie had no problem with what I wanted to ask Yvette, so I sent the text expressing Sadie's sentiments about forgiving Yvette, and also my desire to be forgiven by Yvette. In what seemed like an eternity, but in reality, was only a few minutes, I received a text from Yvette, expressing her delight in Sadie's response, and her acceptance of my request to be forgiven. I concluded this miracle moment of forgiveness by thanking Yvette for forgiving me.

I can't begin to tell you how it felt to be free from the weight of needing to be forgiven. I wish it would have come sooner, but I'm so glad it came when it did. I had put off that moment for nearly thirty years, out of the fear of being rejected or misunderstood. For Sadie, Yvette, and me that day represented a defining moment of freedom that had the power to wipe away decades of

> *Just the knowledge you have been forgiven is liberating.*

emotional pain, especially for Yvette and me. Just the knowledge you have been forgiven is liberating to the soul. I continue to walk in the freedom of that moment and pray that Sadie and Yvette know that I thank and appreciate them both for extending me the miracle of being forgiven. Ephesians 4:32 says, "And be kind to one another, tenderhearted, forgiving one another, even as God for Christ's sake has forgiven you."

Uncommon Grace

At this writing, it's been nearly 34 years since that day at Ontario International Airport, when I stood on the curbside with just the clothes on my back. That was "day one" of the long road to restoration Sadie and I have been traveling. I can honestly say that we both have come a mighty long way.

Sadie is my best friend, and the person I am blessed to grow old with. Even when Sadie was diagnosed with breast cancer, and had to endure a series of chemotherapy treatments, we seemed to grow even closer. I watched as she handled the pain, nausea, and very difficult physical discomfort. Through it all, I never heard Sadie complain even once. She had every right to protest what was happening to her, but she handled it all with uncommon grace. Her faith in God never wavered during all that she was experiencing.

I remember when, after losing most of her hair, she decided to purchase a wig. Sadie has always had long flowing hair, and I know it was disheartening to lose it, but she never let her disappointment show. The day she wore her wig for the first time, I asked her if I could take her picture. Although I was a little sad, Sadie posed with a big beautiful smile on her face. That really touched me, and that photo remains my screensaver to this day.

When Sadie initially shared with me that she had been diagnosed with cancer, I was devastated and the first emotion I experienced was a heavy heart for Sadie, followed by a gnawing sense of fear. We decided to split up the duties of telling our children about Sadie's battle with cancer. Sadie was tasked with telling Michelle.

I was to give the news to Latoya, and we both would tell our son, Dwight. They all took the news with great sadness. After we told Dwight, he walked into the bathroom, and we could hear him crying deeply. Dwight would break the news to our six grandchildren, and as expected they took it very hard.

Of course, it's no surprise that Sadie received an abundance of support from her family and those who knew she was dealing with cancer. Our children were extremely supportive and always showed their love and concern for what Sadie was going through. There is no question that Sadie's battle with cancer served to bring us closer together as a couple. She allowed me to assist her when needed, and I found myself being more sensitive to her needs and the many doctor appointments on her calendar. Even after her mastectomy, Sadie's attitude remained positive and upbeat. Watching her take everything in stride caused me to complain less about my little aches and pains when I compared them to what she was experiencing.

The good news is that on January 18, 2020, Sadie achieved one-year cancer-free, by the grace of God! She is very active, and her beautiful hair is starting to make a comeback. She is always on the go and seems to have an even brighter outlook on life. She has a few ongoing small discomforts, but as time goes by, she is over-coming them one by one, and taking life on one day at a time. We are both so grateful to all those who prayed and encouraged us both through Sadie's ordeal. We give God the glory for the great things He has done for us over the years.

Sixteen

The Miracle Bible Story

T HE STORY I'M ABOUT to share is a true account of what I
consider a restoration miracle. In 1983, two years after Sadie and
I were separated, I was living in the Acorn Apartments in Oakland.
I was on a Section 8, government rent subsidy program where the
amount of the rent subsidy was based on your income. Because
I didn't have any income, I was in a "zero" rent status. There was
always a lot of drug activity in these apartments, heroin, crack and
powder cocaine were the drugs of choice for many people. About a
year into my Section 8 contract, I went through an eviction process
and had to move. I still can't figure out how I managed to be evicted
from a "zero" rent apartment, but that's exactly what happened.

I remember coming down to the day before the sheriff's lock-
out would take place. Lockouts consisted of the sheriff making sure
the premises were vacant, subsequently allowing the locks to be
changed, and posting signs warning against reentry. If anything
remained in the apartment, I would be unable to remove it. I also
recall things being scattered all over the floor and eventually leaving
most of it right where it was. Once I was gone there was no coming
back for anything. I managed to put what I could in storage and
kept it moving.

A few weeks later I ran into one of my former neighbors from the Acorn Apartments who came up to me and said, "You know, I helped them clean out your apartment, and you know what?" I said, "No, what?" and she said, "You didn't even take your Bible." When she said that, I just gave her a blank stare, not really understanding why she needed to tell me that. For reasons that will become clear, I never forgot what she said, and how she said it. I just kept on living a destructive lifestyle, using and selling drugs. The year was 1983.

Now let's fast forward to 2007, I have been back home with my wife and children for twenty-one years, I am drug-free, back in the real estate business, living in a nice home, and serving God. So, I was going about my business when I received a call from my friend Pastor Albert Featherstone who informed me that a mutual friend, Pastor Don Jones, who I had met 16 years into my recovery, wanted me to know that he had my Bible. Since I had recently spoken at his church in Richmond, California, I assumed he was referring to the study Bible I had while at his church. I told Featherstone that I would get the Bible on my next trip to Northern California.

Before I could make it back up north, about a year later, I received another phone call from Pastor Featherstone, who said, "Dwight, I'm coming down to Southern California to speak at Chino Men's Prison, and I'm going to bring your Bible with me. I thought to myself, "Here we go again with this Bible." So, I asked him to describe the Bible to me. He said, "Dwight, it's a big family Bible!" I said, "What?" He said, "It's got your name written in it, it's got your son's name in it, and some military information. Dwight, this is your family Bible." I couldn't believe what I was hearing. I said, "Featherstone, that's the Bible I left in that apartment, back in 1983. That was about twenty-five years ago. Where did Pastor Jones get that Bible?" I couldn't believe that it really was the family Bible I left in that apartment. Still in disbelief, I said, "I got to call Pastor Jones."

After getting Pastor Jones' number from Featherstone, I called him immediately. When Pastor Jones answered the phone, I said, "Pastor where did you get my Bible?" He said that his mother, who had died three years earlier, worked for the Housing Authority and had to commute from San Francisco to Oakland. She would often stop in the Goodwill or Salvation Army stores, and that she must have purchased the Bible and bought it home after one of her trips to Oakland. He said that he was going through some of her belongings and ran across the Bible. I then explained to Pastor Jones that I had

I am drug-free, back in the real estate business, living in a nice home, and serving God.

left that Bible in an apartment over twenty-five years ago. Before hanging up the phone, we both agreed that it was nothing short of a miracle that the Bible was returned to Sadie and me. I also thanked him for the part he played in returning the Bible to us.

The next day Pastor Featherstone met me at Margaret's home in Moreno Valley. He got out of the car carrying the Bible, walked over, and had handed it to me. Sure enough, it was the family Bible that Sadie and I purchased when we were living in San Diego over thirty years earlier. It was as if I had seen someone raised from the dead. How was it possible that after leaving the Bible in the apartment, and a cleaning crew gathers the Bible up with the other things left behind, and then takes it to the local Goodwill or Salvation Army. Once there it was placed on a shelf as inventory for customers to consider buying. Then, of all the people in Oakland who could have bought that Bible, the only one who decided to purchase it was, Willa Dean Jones, the Godly mother of Pastor Don Jones, a man that I wouldn't meet for another 16 years. I even had a chance to meet Mother Jones when I spoke at her son's church and had no idea that our family Bible was being kept and preserved in her home. Even after her passing in 2005, the Bible would sit for another two years before being discovered by Pastor Jones. All I can say is thank God for Willa Dean Jones!

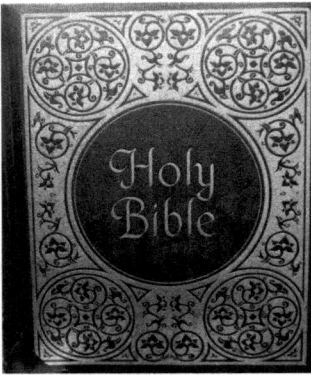

Our Miracle Family Bible was left behind in 1983 and recovered 25 years later in 2008.

After taking the Bible in to show my sister Margaret, I asked that no one tell Sadie about us getting our Bible back. Our 38th wedding anniversary was coming up in a few days, and I decided to wait until then to show Sadie our Family Bible. In the meantime, I found a special case to put the Bible in. On the day of our anniversary, Sadie and I went to a nice restaurant, had dinner, and returned home. When we got there, I asked Sadie to come sit on the couch next to me and let her know that I had something to tell her. She gave me a puzzled look and wondered what I was up to. I broke the suspense and said, "Remember that big family Bible we bought when we lived in San Diego." She said, "Yes." I then told her the whole story of how we got our Family Bible back.

Psalm 23

I reached over and removed the Bible from the case and sat it in her lap. Sadie began laying her hands on the Bible and looking it over. I also opened it up so she could see what was written in the front of the Bible. I showed her the written information that let Pastor Jones know that it was our Bible. As I was talking to her, I noticed that she was holding the white ribbon that's used to mark a place in the Bible. So, I asked her why she was holding on to the ribbon? She said, "Dwight, when we had this Bible in San Diego, I always made sure that this ribbon was in the place marking Psalm 23." We opened the Bible, and the miracle is that after over thirty years, and all that the Bible had gone through, that white ribbon was still in the place marking the Psalm 23. A clear sign to Sadie that God had not forgotten

Since it's return, our Family Bible has become a symbol of our family restoration.

her heart's desire and the many years of struggles gone by. It was a moment that neither of us will ever forget; because there was no way that either of us could explain how it was possible that our family Bible was returned to us after a twenty-five-year separation.

Since it's return, our Family Bible has become a symbol of our family restoration. We even found a book restoration store in Mentone, California. I took it there and asked if our Family Bible could be restored. The shop owner looked at it and said, "This Bible has been through a lot, and I will do my best to restore it. I also asked him not to move the white ribbon that marked the Twenty-third Psalm. A few weeks later when I came to pick the Bible up, I immediately noticed that the Bible didn't look like what it had been through. It looked clean, shiny, sturdy, and beautifully restored. Amen.

The Pledger Family Restoration photo (Top left Alyssa, Michelle, Dwight II, his wife Melody, Sadie, Latoya with son Christopher, me, Theresa, Bottom left, Joseph, Dwight III, Nephew Darius II, Marayah, and Jaslene, taken in 2017 at the American Legion Hall, Redlands, California. In 2019, two great-grandsons, Ryder and Roland, were welcomed into our family.

Epilogue

THIS BRINGS TO A close this leg of my journey. I hope that my story will serve as a clear illustration of the power of choice. If I had stopped to consider the consequences of taking that first hit of cocaine in my friend's kitchen, I might have avoided many years of misery and regret.

Many who read my story will see it as a warning, others will see it as an example, and some will see it as both. It is a warning that you should do your best to avoid some of the pitfalls I fell victim to. Similarly, it is an example in that you will believe that no matter what twists and turns your life takes, it is possible for you to recover, with the help of the Lord. As you have read, my lifeline was to recognize that I was powerless over my addiction to drugs and that unless I surrendered my weakness to God's strength, I would ultimately be destroyed by it.

I wish I could say that once I became a Christian and quit using drugs, that my life was smooth sailing with no problems, but that would be another "Big Lie". The truth is that once I stopped medicating my problems and issues with drugs and alcohol, I had to deal with life on life's terms. I had to face the fact that drugs were not my only problem; in fact, using drugs was just a symptom of some deeper problems. I had to make peace with a past that wanted to upset my present and sabotage my future.

I had to look at my recovery, not as an event or even a destination, but an ongoing process of transformation. The change had to begin at my innermost being and work itself outward until my behavior and lifestyle became who God created me to be. After thirty-four years in recovery, I can report to you that I have only begun to scratch the surface of becoming who God wants me to be. The work of healing the wounded and damaged mind, body, and soul is a difficult and painful process that takes an abundance of grace, plain truth, and redemptive time.

> *Change had to begin at my innermost being and work itself outward.*

The Pain of Change

Since becoming clean and sober, I have made my share of mistakes, faltered, and failed more times than I care to count. The difference is I have faltered and failed while going forward and remaining in the process of recovery. Overcoming weaknesses and developing new strengths will come at a price. It's called the pain of change, which is far better than the pain of remaining the same. The key is not to get stuck or turn around and go back into the hellhole God pulled you out of. Just remember falling and failing is baked into the human experience, so don't stay there. Please don't beat yourself up, because the blessing is that you are failing your way to success. When you sin against God or transgress the boundaries of family and friends, be quick to ask for forgiveness, and keep moving forward. Get used to it, because you will need to do it often, for a variety of reasons; so don't get tired of doing the right thing for the right reasons.

All of God's creations are in some kind of process of recovery. Everyone you know is encountering some kind of life struggle. The struggle could be mental, emotional, physical, and even spiritual, so don't think you are the only one going through something. Try to remember two things. First, take life on one day at a time. Do all you can with what you have, from the place you are, in the twenty-four hours you have each day. Second, no matter

Be quick to ask for forgiveness, and keep moving forward.

what you are going through, just know that it has not come to stay; it has come to pass. Most of life's struggles have a way of working themselves out sooner or later. The good news is that in the having and the overcoming of our struggles, we grow stronger and gain wisdom in the process.

Finally, it has been my esteemed honor to share with you *The Truth About The Big Lie.* I hope that something you have read will be a source of inspiration that will result in a lasting positive transformation. I will end my story with the words of Jesus Christ, "You shall know the truth, and the truth will make you free... and if the Son shall set you free you will be free indeed."

Dedication

IN THE ORDER OF their transitions, this book is dedicated to the memory of Walter L. Tolson, Luvenia (Roby) Edwards, Pastor Greg D. Williams and to my living family, Sadie T. Pledger, Dwight D. Pledger II, Michelle S. Pledger, Latoya R. (Pledger) Gonzales, all of whom have made, and continue to make an indelible impression on my life in their own unique way.

My uncle, Walter L. Tolson, demonstrated compassion and love for his fellow man throughout his life. He was a strong pillar in our family who always assisted those less fortunate. He was ever ready to lend a helping hand. Even in the closing moments of his life, Walter exhibited love, joy, peace, longsuffering, gentleness, goodness, faith, meekness, and temperance. We miss you "Big Walt."

My mother, Luvenia (Roby) Edwards, nearly gave up her life bringing me into the world. She single-handedly raised seven children. She never stopped praying for us and giving to others. Before her passing, she saw all of her children enter into personal relationships with their God and Savior.

I met my friend and brother in Christ, Greg D. Williams, while we were both walking in darkness, drug-addicted, and headed for destruction. We were both blessed to forsake the darkness and to choose the Light of the World, Jesus Christ. I miss our friendship, but most of all I miss our fellowship and ministry work.

Sadie, my wife of 47 years, is nothing short of amazing. She is a woman of faith, integrity, patience, and longsuffering. She is truly a living example of love, forgiveness, and faithfulness to family and friends.

My son Dwight II is a handsome, intelligent, hard-working husband, father, grandfather, and business owner. Watching my son experience life's highs, lows and everything in between has taught me to wait on God, who will see Dwight II through it all.

My daughter Michelle is a beautiful, intelligent, talented, educator, and speaker, with a zest for life and adventure. Michelle gives me hope for the next generation because she possesses a love and concern for family and a passion for making a difference in the lives of people nationally and internationally.

My daughter Latoya is a beautiful, intelligent, and caring wife, mother, and special education teacher. Latoya is special in that she has a way of knowing what I need to do to solve a variety of issues. She shows her love with acts of kindness and concern for me, as well as others.

Acknowledgments

I'D LIKE TO THANK the original editor, Dr. Paulette Brown Hinds, for her diligence in helping to get the first edition published; my friend, Francis Venegas, for helping with laying the foundation from which this finished project was built; my very gifted niece, Nyika Taylor, who encouraged me to resume the work on this book project after a prolonged delay; and my friend Tamara Williams, for being a sounding board and much needed second set of eyes on the manuscript in its early development and editing process.

Finally, I want to thank my daughter, Dr. Michelle Sadrena Pledger, for her commitment to excellence, editorial support, and for being the driving influence that provoked me to complete this expanded edition.

About the Author

FOR OVER THIRTY YEARS Dwight Pledger has been about the business of developing, fine-tuning, and perfecting his message of hope and restoration to thousands. Dwight's message is not built on the platitudes of other men and women but is born out of a personal journey through a life that has seen him rise to the pinnacle of business success only to fall victim to a destructive habit and waste it all away. Hooked and homeless in 1986, Dwight found himself flat on his back, a broken, wounded, and hurting man, looking up and calling on a power greater than himself; and because he looked up he was able to get up.

In Dwight's autobiography, *The Truth About the Big Lie,* he chronicled a seven-year journey into the world of drug and alcohol addiction. This second edition's updated and expanded content includes the past thirty-four years he has been in recovery. Dwight uses his story to be a warning to would-be addicts, and an example for those who may be struggling with addiction and no longer want to remain in bondage. Dwight also gives valuable insight to those who love someone who is addicted and need to understand what drives their addiction.

From 1992 to 2015 Dwight served as co-founder and president of Ray of Hope Ministries, a drug and alcohol outreach and restoration ministry, based in Southern California. Dwight, along with the Ray of Hope Ministry teams, took their message of hope and healing to churches, prisons, rehabilitation centers, and non-profit organizations. Ray of Hope also established and managed two women's recovery homes in San Bernardino, California, and consulted with many organizations working to establish their own in-house recovery support groups.

In 2003, Dwight officially became a member of the Les Brown Platinum Speaker Program. As a protégée of Les Brown, Dwight has received personal mentoring and has traveled nationally and internationally sharing the stage with Les on numerous occasions. Dwight continues to work and collaborate with Les on many events and projects on an ongoing basis.

For the past eight years, Dwight has joined forces with Dan Smith; together they founded D&D Training and Coaching Solutions. Using their collective insights to develop a training and coaching system known as Three-Dimensional Storytelling (3D). Dwight and Dan are currently co-hosting Les Brown's Monday Motivation Call, where they present a broad range of personal development topics and training modules weekly.

Dwight offers a seven-week coaching program to recovering addicts who want to develop and share their addiction and recovery story. Dwight also conducts Team 3:16 Workshops in which he teaches the attendees how to share their salvation testimony in 3 minutes and 16 seconds or less.

Dwight has three children, seven grandchildren, and two great-grandchildren. He presently resides in Southern California with his wife Sadie, and they have been married for forty-eight years.

Connect with Dwight

Facebook	Dwight Pledger
Twitter	@DwightPledger
Web Site	DwightPledger.com
Email	Dwight@DwightPledger.com

www.ingramcontent.com/pod-product-compliance
Lightning Source LLC
Chambersburg PA
CBHW071958090426
42740CB00011B/1988